Els van Dongen
Ruth Kutalek (Eds.)

# Facing Distress

department of ethnomedicine

# Wiener ethnomedizinische Reihe

herausgegeben von

Unit Ethnomedizin und International Health
Zentrum für Public Health,
Medizinische Universität Wien

Band/Volume 4

LIT

# FACING DISTRESS

## Distance and proximity in times of illness

edited by

Els van Dongen and Ruth Kutalek

LIT

Cover illustration: A Zande healer rubs protective oil on the head of a patient.
Photograph Armin Prinz

**Bibliographic information published by the Deutsche Nationalbibliothek**
The Deutsche Nationalbibliothek lists this publication in the Deutsche Nationalbibliografie; detailed bibliographic data are available in the Internet at http://dnb.d-nb.de.

ISBN 978-3-7000-0622-0 (Austria)
ISBN 978-3-8258-0171-7 (Germany)

**A catalogue record for this book is available from the British Library**


Krotenthallergasse 10/8
A-1080 Wien
Tel. +43 (0) 1 / 409 56 61
Fax +43 (0) 1 / 409 56 97
e-Mail: wien@lit-verlag.at
http://www.lit-verlag.at

LIT VERLAG Dr. W. Hopf
Berlin
Ziegelstr. 30
D-10177 Berlin

**Auslieferung:**
Österreich: Medienlogistik Pichler-ÖBZ GmbH & Co KG
IZ-NÖ, Süd, Straße 1, Objekt 34, A-2355 Wiener Neudorf
Tel. +43 (0) 2236/63 535 - 290, Fax +43 (0) 2236/63 535 - 243, e-Mail: mlo@medien-logistik.at
Deutschland: LIT Verlag Fresnostr. 2, D-48159 Münster
Tel. +49 (0) 2 51/620 32 - 22, Fax +49 (0) 2 51/922 60 99, e-Mail: vertrieb@lit-verlag.de

Distributed in the UK by: Global Book Marketing, 99B Wallis Rd, London, E9 5LN
Phone: +44 (0) 20 8533 5800 – Fax: +44 (0) 1600 775 663
http://www.centralbooks.co.uk/acatalog/search.html

Distributed in North America by:

Transaction Publishers
New Brunswick (U.S.A.) and London (U.K.)

Transaction Publishers
Rutgers University
35 Berrue Circle
Piscataway, NJ 08854

Phone: +1 (732) 445 - 2280
Fax: + 1 (732) 445 - 3138
for orders (U. S. only):
toll free (888) 999 - 6778
e-mail:
orders@transactionspub.com

## Contents

## Introduction

Els van Dongen & Ruth Kutalek

Distance and proximity, distance and involvement, face-to-face, empathy, belonging, compliance and resistance, participation and observation; these at random chosen concepts are the conditions of intersubjectivity and human relationships. The study of these concepts illuminate the nature of social and cultural relationships, the importance of the context of such relationships and the ways people create their identities. Thinking about distance and proximity offers possibilities to think about "we and the other", the making of communities, professionalisation, theories or methodologies. Historically, anthropologists have debated the problematics of concepts such as distance/proximity. These debates vary from the impact of distance/proximity on theory and the production of knowledge to extensive reflections on relationships during fieldwork and differences of gender, age, status, power and position. At present, attention to fieldwork conditions and relationships seems to be more necessary than ever. Events in the field are emotionally intense; issues of policy, poverty and inequality surround the ethnographic practice; tensions, interests and disjunctures weave their way through interactions and colour human practices and perspectives. This is not only so for anthropology. Also in disciplines such as medicine or psychiatry or in social, cultural and political interactions one has to alternate between these two positions, balancing on the thin rope of uncertainty and ambivalence that underlie human relationships. Besides, one has to realise that it is not the anthropologist who determines her place on the continuum of distance and proximity; it is the other or the situation that allows to be proximate or distanced.

Distance and proximity are concepts par excellence to describe what may happen in times of illness and suffering. Usually the concepts are described as if they relate to a fixed point (in time, space or relations), but there seems to be no fixed point. Perhaps we should speak of a "flow". When one faces distress and suffering the need of proximity of the sick or suffering person may manifest itself or – the opposite – a need of distance exists. A doctor or an anthropologist may believe proximity is necessary, but the other can disagree. A patient may be in need to be proximate to others, but the others believe distance is better. This can result in loneliness and desolation. Then there is the question: how proximate or how distanced one must or can be?

Or: when one has to be proximate or not? It is not only that the nature and quality of social relationships can be caught in times of illness and suffering with the two concepts, also the force of distance and proximity manifests itself in times of sickness and suffering and may influence the course of "events".

Illness raises questions for all individuals. The sick individual will question his/her relationship with others and being-in-the-world. In his book *The body silent* Murphy describes the heroic struggle between the sick and suffering on the one hand and the others who take care of them and in the final chapter he gives a description of what proximity and distance is perhaps about: "There is, then, a constant process built into all our endeavours in which we must reach out, relate, and love, while taking care not to lose ourselves. [...] In the final analysis, social life is made possible by keeping a delicate balance between falling inward and falling outward. The structure of all our moments is that we are constantly being pulled apart between the two. It is also the story of our lives." (Murphy 1990: 227).

Not only to family members, friends, anthropologists and others proximity and distance is a delicate balance, also in relationship with others, such as doctors or healers. A sick person can experience empathy and compassion, but also conflict and struggle. The doctor also can. Winckler's novel *La maladie de Sachs* illustrates how a doctor may be ruined when he is "too close" to his patients. In fact, finding a balance lies at the heart of human experience, in "forms of resistance in the life course, in social relations, in biophysical processes", which in turn means an emergence "of what is shared in [...] human condition: loss, deprivation, oppression, pain" (Kleinman 1995: 119). It is often argued that professional transformations of suffering delegitimate patients' suffering and moral commentaries. Therefore, Kleinman (1995) looks for an ethnography of interpersonal experience. In such an ethnography – or medical practice – doctors and patients share the experiences of this human condition.

There is a difference in the meaning of distance and proximity for anthropologists and doctors. This difference directs attention to the relation between empathy and the production of knowledge. The idea of a relationship between empathy (closely related to distance and proximity) and knowledge production seems "utilistic" and calculating. However, one is not only confronted with the problem of the "creation of the other" by ethnographies or medical reports, but also with the conditions that make distance and proximity possible or impossible. The alternation between proximity and distance means becoming involved in the suffering of others (proximity) and witnessing the effects and consequences of historical, political and social processes that caused the suffering or made it worse (distance). This, in turn, can cause moral dilemmas for both, the anthropologist/doctor and the sufferer. It will influence the precarious balance one has found between proximity and distance and leave the anthropologist or doctor with the question if their discipline has to be a science of consequences (Reynolds Whyte 2005) and responsibility. The answer to such a question is not a simple one. A science of consequence and responsibility requires that an anthropologist or a doctor makes a choice to take a position. To take a position means to be proximate to the one and to be more distant to the other… When people face distress issues of distance and proximity become urgent. It seems that there is no way to escape a choice of a position along the continuum; anthropologists, doctors and patients are all involved in this struggle.

The authors of this volume take up issues of distance and proximity in illness and suffering in various situations. The papers were first discussed in a workshop *Facing distress. Distance and proximity in times of illness* at the 8th Biennial EASA (European Association of Social Anthropologists) conference in Vienna in September 2004. We believed that the issues discussed at that time needed further reflection and elaboration.

Sylvie Fainzang in "Anthropology and medicine: Empathy, experience and knowledge" relates the concept of empathy to proximity and argues that empathic relationships between anthropologists and informants on the one hand, and those between doctors and patients on the other are not the same. In a new way, Sylvie Fainzang takes up the classical dilemma of proximity and distance in anthropological work (see for example Malinowski 1967). In a classic doctor-patient relationship, instruments are helpful to the doctor to distance himself from the patient. Anthropologists have to make an effort in doing so. Drawing on various case studies, Sylvie Fainzang shows the difference in nature and role of empathy in medicine and anthropology. Her conclusion is that anthropologists can benefit from empathy when they are able to control it and to distance themselves. According to the author, the anthropologist must be able to understand different others, a process, which requires distancing oneself from an informant. Besides, Sylvie argues, it is often overlooked that an anthropologist cannot develop empathic relationships with everyone. She regards empathy as an intellectual construction and of heuristic value for research. Her conclusion is that empathy is the condition and the illusion of knowledge.

In “The other’s pain is the anthropologist’s strain”, Els van Dongen discusses how proximity in fieldwork has become problematic. Situations in the field have changed and the classical alternation of distance and proximity is disturbed by situations, contexts, interests of informants and anthropologists. Many anthropologists work in areas where violence has become a common feature of people’s daily lives. In such situations the first part of the pair participant-observation often have become impossible for various reasons, while the technique of observation may cause moral dilemmas for the anthropologist. Closeness and distance is not a neatly controlled process; in fact, ethnographers may become entangled in politics of power, politics of forgetting, politics of positioning, etc. that lie beyond their and their informants scope and power, but nevertheless have a deep impact on their relationship, involvement and proximity and thus on the production of anthropological knowledge. Els argues that both, informants and anthropologists are moral beings with responsibility. Much medical anthropological work today needs collaborative thinking and reflections on its consequences, but it also needs moral confidence and thus proximity-with-distance.

Working in Congo and Tanzania, Ruth Kutalek and Armin Prinz in their contribution “Witchcraft and violence: Aspects of distance and proximity”, discuss their personal apprehension to this topic and their feelings of helplessness when they observed friends, informants and their relatives accused of being a witch. They ask the question of how to react as an anthropological researcher when confronted with witchcraft and discuss several cases to show how it affects people’s day-to-day lives and causes suffering. The authors also show that proximity plays its role in witchcraft: the closer a person socially is, the easier is bewitchment. But also spatial proximity is important. According to the authors, this is one of the reasons why, for example, the Zande prefer to live in homesteads that lie in a certain distance from each other. Witchcraft used to strengthen kinship ties, but at present it has weakened those ties in dramatic ways. Witchcraft rapidly changes. Ruth and Armin also discuss a recent phenomenon: child witches. Besides, they argue that witchcraft cannot be understood without taking into account the economic, political and social uncertainties. Poverty often is the underlying cause for witchcraft accusations. The authors show that witchcraft and violence cause a complex dynamic social process, in which people try to establish a new equilibrium between proximity and distance. This process nowadays is often characterised by severe violence towards the – often elderly, female witch.

Annemiek Richters et al. in their contribution "Face to face with refugee women's distress in the Netherlands: Distance and proximity in the aftermath of sexual violence" explore how distance and proximity can be used to gain a better understanding of what refugee women have to go through in the aftermath of sexual violence. They provide material from their four studies in this field and show how political, legal, economic, social, and cultural variables shape distancing and approximation processes. They present the reader some of the health consequences of sexual violence towards women, in particular the psychological consequences that relate to distance and proximity. It becomes clear that it is not only the immediate psychological distress that forces women to remain silent about what happened; shame, taboo and guilt surrounding the subject also causes this silence, as well as social atrocities they might have to suffer. Coming too close to the women's experience would then cause more distress. However, in asylum procedures, the distancing tactics of officials may prevent women from telling about these experiences that could be a ground for granting the refugee status. The officials' attitude, however, is paradoxical, because they expect women to reveal things that can only be told in an atmosphere of trust and proximity. In medical examinations and treatment during the appeal process, doctors and psychiatrists underline the importance of a safe environment for the client. At the same time they are reluctant to encourage the disclosure of sexual assault, fearing negative consequences for their clients. Victims do not have many possibilities to overcome their fear of disclosure and the Dutch government can get away with refusal to look at medical evidence of sexual assault. One of the researchers, Marian Tankink, also found silence and fear of disclosure in the women's daily lives. Cultural censorship and gossip will keep women at a distance to their husbands and social groups. Researchers themselves are struggling with distance and proximity in cases of sexual violence, as do therapists. Although it is known that trust, safety and proximity are important for therapy and the well-being of women, careful consideration of how proximate or distanced one should be is as important.

Charlotte Jacobsen in her contribution "Working towards proximity" shows that proximity of staff to patients in a forensic psychiatric ward means work. Proximity is an aspiration but also a tool to make relationships with patients. The staff is caught in a paradox, which seems to be common in such relations (see also Van Dongen 2004): one the one hand, the relation is characterised by intersubjectivity and on the other, proximity is challenged by patients who often resort. Also patients struggle with proximity and distance in their relationships with the staff. With ethnographic data from a forensic psychiatric ward Charlotte shows that knowing in the sense of obtaining a feeling determines the staff's access and proximity to patients. To be near to a patient is "to have good contact", which is necessary to get into the "inside" of the patients. Social and cultural dynamics in the ward may trigger proximity.

Jónína Einirsdótter in "Parents' first encounter with their preemie: Distance or devotion?" discusses the dilemmas and choices people make when they "meet" their premature born babies. These are the dilemmas of closeness and distance. She shows that maternal bonding and thus proximity to the newborn has not be taken for granted. Starting with the work of Scheper-Hughes (1992) and Hrdy (1999), who question the idea that bonding with the child is a "natural" issue, Jónína describes the first encounter of the father and mother with their newborn child. Fathers sometimes are the first to meet their children, because the mother is in intensive care or not able to go to the neonatal ward. The reader then is confronted with the dilemma of the father, who often wants to be close to his wife but feels responsible to provide news about the baby to his wife and family members. The fluidity of proximity and distance is expressed in the attempts to satisfy all. When parents see their child for the first time, their reactions may differ from distance to devotion or both at the same time. Jónína argues that one should not take the "natural bond" between mother and child for granted; mothers (and fathers) become attached to their child in their own way.

Josep Comelles approaches the issue of proximity and distance from a totally different angle. In "Feelings, distance and emotions in medical practice" he shows how doctors and others produce rhetoric on doctor-patient relationships, and thereby build the ideal type of the "good doctor" that contradicts the type common in the hegemonic medical model. Those (first) relationships are characterised by the need of distance, represented by clinical examination and the need for proximity of the professionals with their patients in the management of pain and sentiments. Josep Comelles shows the complexity of this issue by exploring different medical settings in today's medical practice and in the past. He highlights the medical rhetoric about positivistic strategies to gather signs and symptoms and to develop diagnostic tools. Josep concludes that when doctors work in other places of the world than they were trained, and arrive in a slum or work for a NGO that is engaged in a Third World country, they will likely ask themselves what their professional identity should be, that of the type of the hegemonic model or the doctor who is proximate and empathic to his patients and their family members.

**References**

Hrdy, S. B.

1999 *Mother nature: A history of mothers, infants, and natural selection.* New York: Pantheon Books.

Kleinman, A.

1995 *Writing at the margin. Discourse between anthropology and medicine.* Berkeley: University of California Press.

Malinowski, B.

1967 *A diary in the strict sense of the term.* Stanford, California: Stanford University Press (text: Valetta Malinowska).

Murphy, R.

1990 *The body silent.* New York, London: Norton.

Reynolds Whyte, S.

2005 Uncertain undertakings: Practicing health care in the subjunctive mood. In: V. Steffen, R. Jenkins & H. Jessen (eds), *Managing uncertainty. Ethnographic studies of illness, risk and the struggle for control.* Copenhagen: Museum Tusculanum Press, pp. 245-265.

Scheper-Hughes, N.

1992 *Death without weeping: The violence of everyday life in Brazil.* Berkeley: University of California Press.

Van Dongen, E.

2004 *Worlds of psychotic people. Wanderers, 'bricoleurs', strategists.* New York, London: Routledge.

Winckler, Martin

1998 *La maladie de Sachs*. Paris: Editions J'ai lu.

# Anthropology and medicine: Empathy, experience and knowledge

Sylvie Fainzang

At the heart of the methodological and epistemological reflection involved in anthropological practice lies the following question: To what extent is empathy coextensive to the anthropological approach? In other words, is the practice of the profession contingent on empathy, generally conceived of as the ability to put oneself in the place of the Other? This is also a key question in the more particular context of medical anthropology, in so far as it constructs objects and conducts field research in which the anthropologist has a particular relationship with individuals, their ailments and their bodies – an area traditionally occupied by medicine.

Just as anthropologists' relationship with their informants cannot be likened to that of doctors with their patients, so the empathic dimension characteristic of both types of relationship differs in each case[1]. The aim of this paper is to examine the connection between empathy and knowledge and, more precisely, the specific role that empathy is likely to play, in anthropology, in the process of knowledge production. Are empathy and knowledge characteristic of a relationship of possibility or one of necessity? What is the added value of the empathic dimension and of the phenomena traditionally associated with it in anthropological research (experience, emotion, understanding through emotion, etc.)?

Based on examples drawn from various field studies, I undertake a cross-cutting analysis of the nature and role of empathy in the contexts of the doctor-patient and the observer-informant relationships, and evaluate the part that empathy plays in producing a form of knowledge towards which both types of relationship tend. In concrete terms, I examine the way and the conditions in which the empathic relationship can be established, with a view to furthering insight into the knowledge-creation project of anthropology. This perspective on these different types of empathy and the examination of these diverse situations help me to answer the following questions: What are the implications of empathy on the anthropologist's work and what is its heuris-

---

[1] The idea here is not to compare what happens between the anthropologist and his or her informant, on the one hand, with the identification that doctors are likely to have with their patients during psychotherapeutic or psycho-analytical treatment, on the other. On this point see Stein (1980) who in this regard examines the concepts of transfer and counter-transfer and the conditions of their applicability.

tic value? In other words, what impact does empathy have on the production of knowledge and in what conditions does the former facilitate the latter?

## Empathy in the doctor-patient relationship

The first question we need to consider is whether it is necessary for doctors to have an empathic relationship with their patients in order to understand and treat them. This question has no simple answer because it immediately raises many others. First, do doctors need to understand their patients in order to treat them? What does "understand" actually mean in this case? What are the implications, for the doctor, of having an empathic relationship? Does it mean that they have to identify with their patients? And in order to do so, do they need to have shared their experience? Do they need to have (or to have had) the same disease in order to be considered as "a good doctor"? Most doctors would say "of course not". Their diagnosis and treatment do not require a sharing of the patient's suffering or the doctor's ability to put him- or herself in the patient's position. But is this how patients and some doctors actually see things? On this subject it is fruitful to examine empathy from the point of view of both the patient and the healer (a doctor or not) in different cultural contexts, before proposing an ethnological reading of what these perceptions reveal.

In the Bisa society, a West African lineal society, the therapeutic function is fulfilled by traditional healers. Two types of healer exist. The first type, in the majority, acquire their knowledge from their ancestors (agnatic or uterine lineage), from their father in the case of men and from their mother in that of women. The second type, the minority, become healers of a particular illness because they themselves had it in the past. This process of acquisition of therapeutic knowledge is an exception to the prevailing principle of genealogical transmission. It has the effect of training healers with a single speciality, able to heal an illness in which they have experience. The justification is then that it is necessary to have known the disease to be able to recognize and understand the patient. Due to the requirement of having been in the patient's position in order to be able to heal him or her, this is a perfect example of the idea of knowledge through experience and empathy. Even if their legitimacy is not superior to that of the healers from whom they inherited their function, it is at least equal as regards the institution. Here experience replaces learning through transmission and gives the healer the ability to understand the patient and the power to heal him or her (Fainzang 1986).

In the very different cultural context of former drinkers in Western societies, the subjects consider that only another alcoholic can really understand an alcoholic. At Vie libre (an association of former alcoholics) one has to have personally experienced the "alcoholic's illness" to understand it and to be able to treat others (Fainzang, 1996). In this respect, the healer's role is more readily recognized in peers (other former "alcoholic patients") than in medical doctors. Although this phenomenon is characteristic of most organizations of this nature, there is divergence in the definition of the nature and subject of the experience. For instance, Alcoholics Anonymous and Vie libre have distinctly different conceptions of the idea of sharing an experience and the possibility of identification. The former believe that only alcoholics can understand, whereas at Vie libre the alcoholics' spouses, who have experienced the disease by suffering through life with an alcoholic, are called on to share the healing experience and are considered capable of sharing their suffering. (Alcoholics' spouses often claim to be former alcoholics or former patients when they visit alcoholics in hospital to try to persuade them to join the movement. The idea is that the treatment will be more effective if there is greater understanding.) A second difference concerns the group's relationship with the medical profession. Alcoholics Anonymous has a clear-cut position in this respect: they believe that there is no point in consulting doctors since they are not themselves alcoholics and are therefore unable to understand a heavy drinker. The Vie libre movement has a slightly different approach: it recommends cooperation with the medical profession even if it believes that true healing of an alcoholic is possible only among former alcoholics. Cooperation with doctors is considered necessary in so far as certain patients need detoxification treatment, even if it is insufficient. The real healing is achieved by being with those who are (or can imagine themselves) in the alcoholic's position. Most doctors agree; they consider these organizations to be useful and beneficial, and readily refer their patients to them, especially to Vie libre, as a complement to the detoxification cure. Their motto is: "We cure you, and You heal" – plagiarizing Ambroise Paré's famous formula "I dressed him, and God healed him". This tendency to see certain individuals' ability to understand and to feel what someone else is experiencing as a sign of a superior competence in the field of therapeutic care, is nevertheless problematical. Certain members of the movement who feel that they have been vested with the role of a "healer" sometimes recommend therapeutic solutions to other alcoholics, when in fact this would normally be the doctor's role. For instance, they recommend taking esperal[2] or antidepressants that they themselves took in a situation they see as similar. Although some may qualify this as abusive, it is interesting to note that it is the competence endowed by empathy that prevails and prompts alcoholic peers to recommend treatment, regardless of medical advice. The link is nevertheless clearly expressed here between experience, empathy and knowledge. Like the African healers considered to be able to cure a disease that they themselves have had, intimate knowledge of the disease and the possibility of identifying with the patient is believed to endow a person with superior competencies for overcoming the disease. It is as if, in the medical relationship, the healers' empathy, their understanding of their patients and their identification with them, through their personal experience of the disease, were an alternative to learning and equipped them with competence that was not identical but equal.

A third situation examined here is that of doctors, observed during their consultations (in French hospitals), and their relationship with their patients around certain pathologies. Various types of empathy can emerge in the practice of their profession, two of which seem to be dominant. The first type of empathy is induced by a specific illness that the doctor may or may not have had, for which he or she developed a particular interest, and that may even prompt him or her to choose the speciality corresponding to it. This is the case, for example, of a lung specialist who is very understanding with his asthmatic patients because he also suffers from asthma. It is very similar to the case of African healers considered above; only the learning process is different. While observing consultations we noted that doctors sometimes reveal this information to patients who seem reluctant to take their advice and the drugs prescribed. In this way the patient is informed that the doctor is familiar with the problem. The patient's attitude then changes, as if intimate knowledge of the illness and the resulting empathy reinforced the doctor's understanding and therefore his or her competence.

The other type of empathy is induced by the doctor's ability or tendency to identify with a patient because he or she sees him- or herself in that specific patient. Either the patient is of the same age or gender as the doctor, or the patient is a child or an aged person in whom the doctor sees his or her own child or parents. Empathy can also be experienced with someone close to the

---

[2] Esperal is a substance (*disulfiram*) whose properties have the effect of making any subsequent ingestion of alcohol extremely unpleasant. Generally administered in the form of tablets taken daily, it produces what is known as the anti-abuse effect, a set of physical reactions such as congestion of the face, tachycardia, vomiting and low blood pressure.

patient such as a family member. In all cases it stems from a tendency to see oneself through another person. Yet the question of the outcome of the relationship of proximity generated by empathy remains unanswered. Does it produce better understanding of the illness and a greater ability of curing it?

While medical empathy helps to establish a relationship of trust, there is no doubt that it can also be productive. For instance, it may allow the doctor to collect information required for diagnostic purposes and perhaps also to obtain stricter compliance by the patient, for we know that a patient's compliance is improved when there is a relationship of trust with his or her doctor (Haynes, Taylor & Sackett 1979). Questioning the role of empathy in medical practice, Spiro et al. (1993) wonder whether it is dangerous for a patient if a doctor becomes too empathic. The authors unanimously answer in the negative. Empathy is fundamentally good in so far as it provides the doctor with information on the patient and can produce something good in the relationship, if only because it influences the patient's feelings towards the doctor. Is this trust contingent on empathy? It does not seem that the possibility of being seen as a good doctor (and actually being one) necessarily requires empathy. Although empathy can be useful and may even compensate for or enhance competence, it is not essential. It may have a technical role or function but it does not enter into the definition of healing, neither in clinical methods nor in therapeutic care. Medical em

pathy facilitates access to knowledge that doctors need to obtain on their patients, but it is not a condition on which the practice of their profession depends. Conversely, proximity with patients (e.g. family proximity, that certain doctors refuse), does not preclude the ability to analyse a case, at least in somatic medicine: certain doctors' choice not to treat their own family members relates either to the emotional charge of this type of situation, to the difficulty of taking decisions (e.g. an operation or chemotherapy), to the psychological or moral pressure that they are likely to experience, or, finally, to family and friends' judgement of their acts. Although empathy is not a prerequisite, it is neither an obstacle to knowledge[3].

---

[3] Empathy may nevertheless be an obstacle to the adoption of adequate behaviour from a therapeutic point of view. This is the conclusion of Snow (2000) who describes a case in which a doctor's excessive empathy with a patient is seen as preventing him from administering appropriate treatment in an emergency.

## Empathy in the anthropological field

Generally considered as intrinsic to ethnological field work, empathy is a complex attitude or disposition. It is not always clear whether it is related to the observer or to the object studied. How is this empathy constructed? Is it a necessary or useful tool? Is it deliberate or inevitable? Is it controlled?

In this section I examine the conditions in which empathy can or must exist. I question the connection between the existence of empathy and the type of research (the object, the group, the research question), with a view to establishing what this empathy contributes to the knowledge project. For this purpose I draw on some personal experiences in the field and, above all, on a study on African polygamy in immigrant families. In this research project I investigated the way in which women deal with their sexuality and their reproductive capacity in the context of this type of marriage in France, and the future of polygamy in situations of immigration. The method employed was maximum immersion in the field, which involved spending long days with these women, in their homes, helping them to prepare meals, feeding their babies when they were busy, or going shopping with them. In this way I was able to experience – albeit only partly – the woman's condition in this type of household.

The first problem was that of the criteria of empathy. It was very difficult to identify (among those who enabled me to feel what they were feeling, or to "put myself in their shoes") the decisive criteria that allow empathy. Even if my empathic relationship with African women was facilitated by the fact that I am also a woman (which is what some of them thought since a person's definition in their society is based primarily on gender), it was nevertheless probably limited, as was my ability to really understand them because I am neither African nor married in a polygamous system (which is what others thought). Hence, there are not simple criteria on which identification can be based, but a set of entangled positions that combine or cancel one another out, making the definition of an optimum position for the realization of empathy an eminently complex affair. We thus see to what extent the construction of empathy is relative, as is that which serves to consolidate it. Is it a question of sensitivity to the difficult material and social conditions in which immigrants live? Is it the possibility of sharing feelings experienced by women married to the same man? Does the social condition of a woman suffice for this empathy to exist or is it necessary to add the experience of particular emotions?

On this point it is relevant to mention what Max Weber (1971) says in the first pages of his book *Economie et société* on the methodological foundations of sociology, where he examines the modes of understanding behaviours and social activity, showing that it can be either rational or empathic (that is, emotional). Yet he shows the limits of understanding in the latter case since the phenomena can be radically different from our own perceptions (or what he calls our "evaluations"). He takes the example of certain religious or mystical phenomena that may be difficult to understand for someone who is inaccessible to this type of experience. According to Weber, when it comes to understanding through empathy, we understand behaviours, reactions or feelings (jealousy, anger, fear, etc.) only to the extent that we are ourselves accessible to those emotions and that they constitute significant entities for us. In a sense, rational understanding is seen to offset the lack of understanding through empathy, which is considered to be productive from the outset.

However, being able to feel what individuals feel, to put oneself in their place, can also be problematical. In this respect I wish to revert briefly to the case of the African women mentioned above, and to report some ethnographic findings. Despite the cramped conditions in which African immigrant families – that are often large – live in France, separation between the sexes persists. The female sphere remains associated with the private domain and the male sphere with the public domain. Consider the case of a family living in Paris in two rooms, each situated on a different floor of an old building in the 20th arrondissement. The smallest room serves as a bedroom for the children and those wives who are not assigned to sexual services. The largest room ($13m^2$) is where all the members of the family meet at mealtimes, especially when visitors are present, and in which the domestic space is restructured on the public/private model. This family comprises a man, his three wives and their twelve children. The furniture in the room consists of three beds arranged in a U-shape (the base of the U against the back wall). The women are seated towards the inside (at the base of the U, against the wall at the end of the room) and the men towards the outside of the U, closer to everything connected with the outside world: the entrance door, the TV set near the door and the telephone, placed on the TV. The public/private opposition is coupled with an outside/inside opposition, also found in the respective positions of the man and the woman when they are in bed. In relation to the opening of the room, the woman always lies behind the man. This occupation of space is significant: women are placed towards the inside not only because they are responsible for domestic work but also because their access to the outside world is controlled and mediated by men. The place assigned to them in the room reflects and symbolizes the position granted to them as regards both the outside world and public life. The husband occupies a strategic intermediate position, between the woman and the door; he is the gateway to the outside world or to society (Fainzang & Journet 1988).

Reference to this situation has the particular advantage of showing how empathy can be constructed and revealed through use of the space in which the ethnological relationship is situated, where "putting oneself in the place of" is fully meaningful, both literally and metaphorically. In fact, my presence was incorporated into this process on the basis of the place that I occupied in their view. Invested with the status of a foreigner, a "visitor", I was initially invited to sit at one of the ends of the U formed by the three beds (that serve both as bed and as seats). In other words, I was seated among the men because I was associated with the outside world. But as the bonds became stronger I lost the status of a representative of the institution (I was neither a social worker likely to provide them with decent accommodation nor an official checking whether they had a valid residence permit). Consequently, I also lost the status of a foreigner. I simply became a woman, a friend of the family who was given a place at the base of the U (either on the bed at the back, or on the most distant part of the lateral beds), that is, among the women. I was not the one who, through my ethnological inquiry, wanted to put myself in the women's place to understand them, but I was effectively put in the women's place. Almost against my will my informants put me in an absolutely empathic position, not only socially but also spatially, that is, both in the context of social relations and in the domestic space.

This immersion and the resulting empathy entail difficulties related to the fact that the observer is unwittingly involved, by the subjects themselves, in their relationships – to the point of finding him- or herself in one camp or another in the event of conflict. This inevitably raises the question of whether one can be in an empathic relationship simultaneously with two individuals in conflict. In the case described here, considering the rivalry between co-spouses inherent in the polygamous situation, it was impossible for me, in the family's eyes, to be the confidant of all concerned. The fact of developing a relationship with a woman and being considered by the family as "her friend" meant that I implicitly supported her in her rivalry with her co-spouse. It followed that I was unable to form a close relationship with the latter. If one confided in me regarding her problems of sterility that she imputed (like all reproduction-related diseases) to persecution by the co-spouse, it stood to reason that the other spouse would not also confide in me. In short, due to the empathy I felt for the first spouse, I was considered unable to put myself in the place of the second one. I consequently had to undertake a painstaking process of reconstruction, consisting in putting together the pieces and compensating for my shortcomings regarding the experience of the second wife in families where I had privileged relations with the first, by striving to build up privileged relations with the second or third wife in other homes. Although empathy was achieved through a long period of frequentation of these women, I experienced the need to withdraw from these situations in order to avoid confining myself to the women's point of view. Not only did I not want to limit myself to understanding the viewpoint of the first wife and not the others (whose social position, via their rank in the order of marriages, is attended by a different way of conceiving of their relations with others, with their husband and with the community at large); I also wanted to avoid limiting my understanding to women only. I wished to understand the social pressure that forces men to take several wives and, within the social relations implicit in this institution, the distress it sometimes causes them.

For the most objective analysis possible of the situation under study, the ability to identify with some, in the process of familiarity of the inquiry, should not stop us from understanding and possibly of also developing empathy for the others, those considered by the former to be their rivals. In rigorous ethnological practice researchers should be able to feel empathy for different individuals in different situations. In this way they are in a position to analyse the power struggles and behavioural logics of the subjects under study. Empathy, inherent in the object and the approach, is therefore something ethnologists have to be able to withdraw from at some point in time. This is necessary in order to be able to "put themselves in the place of" the different informants involved in a play of social relations in which none have exactly the same place, and to be able to stand back from their representations, for analytical purposes.

In this respect, in the research mentioned above on Alcoholics Anonymous, I found myself, from the outset, in the difficult position in which the people studied asked me if I had an alcoholic in my family or if I was concerned in one way or another by the problem, in order to be able to understand them. In all honesty I answered "no" since I have never experienced alcoholism myself nor the suffering induced by the fact of living with an alcoholic. In terms of the categories defined by the organization itself, which distinguishes between "former drinkers", "voluntary abstainers" and "sympathizers", I did not claim to be anything more than a "sympathizer". The term itself put me in a relationship of sympathy and not empathy (a distinction that is worth highlighting and to which I will revert). Yet the members of the branch that I frequented the most regularly asked me to become a "pink card", that is, to have the same status as themselves, the same place, that of a "voluntary abstainer". In short, I found myself snapped up by an object and by people whose pain I had come to understand, intellectually and emotionally, by spending a lot of time with them. But I refused this status, not only because I had no desire to become abstinent but also because it seemed to me imperative to allow myself the means to achieve empathic detachment with a view to coming as close as possible to the truth of the object. In this respect it seems that empathy is a feature not of the ethnologist but of ethnology, in so far as it is not a personal predisposition of the observer but a dimension of his or her approach. Empathy is so closely connected to the ethnologist's approach that it can be achieved without necessarily being sought. It is strongly correlated with the object in so far as it is more easily felt when that object involves emotions (and suffering and disease are strong triggers of emotions), precisely because there is a possibility of identification. I therefore had to try rather to leave the naturally empathic position in which the research put me, and seek the weaknesses in the subjects' behaviours with a view to identifying apparent inconsistencies in some of the observed practices. By putting oneself too much in the place of the subjects studied, and especially remaining there, one runs the risk of entering into their representations to the point of no longer seeing, for instance, that some of their behaviour is paradoxical – a question that ethnology is supposed to investigate. Therefore, I once again felt the need to detach myself from this empathy, although for different reasons to those noted above. Whereas my field research on polygamy raised the question of whom the ethnologist could feel empathy for, considering the multiplicity of places that he or she can occupy in the field, in the case of alcoholics I was confronted with the necessity to find weaknesses, to act as if I was unable to understand them from an emotional point of view, precisely in order to be able to understand them intellectually. Empathy therefore appeared to be a positive stage but one that should last only for a while. Whereas it can be useful to feel empathy, one also has to move beyond it. Hence, empathy can be demanded provided that it is also mastered, allowing one to stand back from it or to deconstruct it.

The question of the bases on which empathy can be realized is crucial when one is working on different types of groups. This was the case, for example, of research that I undertook on the use of medication and medical prescriptions, depending on individuals' religious cultural origin (Catholic, Protestant, Jewish or Muslim) (Fainzang 2001). Here again the question of criteria arises, and these criteria are in a sense always uncertain and sometimes unpredictable. Does the methodological choice of feeling close to people and putting oneself in their place enable one to put oneself in everyone's place? Can the ethnologist put him- or herself in the place of people who are culturally close or, by contrast, different from him or her? What does culturally close mean in this case? Is it a common cultural or religious origin of the ethnologist and his or her informants? Or is it rather the fact of having in common, as in my case, no religious belief at all? The difficulty becomes that of the possibility and viability of empathy in a study that is supposed to be comparative from the outset. If empathy cannot be achieved with everyone, perhaps it would be better to have it with no one (if can be controlled), for nothing enables us a priori to know in which case and with whom, in a heterogeneous population, empathy will have the greatest chances of being felt.

## Empathy and experience

Some people would say that it is impossible to put oneself completely in someone else's place, precisely because one is not in that place. There cannot be complete identification since this move is imagined and not lived. Even when it has an emotional dimension, empathy is always an intellectual construction. And even when it is rooted in experience, it is a theoretical construction. An ethnologist who has experienced neither alcoholism nor the suffering of living with an alcoholic spouse, can still imagine and reconstruct that experience. Empathy is then an intellectual construction.

In Dilthey's definition of empathy as the situation in which "the soul follows the accustomed paths in which it enjoyed and suffered, desired and acted in similar situation" (Dilthey 1959: 219), we see that for him empathy can be experienced only by a person who has lived an identical experience to that of the subject. In other words, one has to have had the same experience to be able to develop an empathic position. Yet, as seen above, it seems that the conditions of the possibility of empathy are as much in an intellectual or emotional position as in the studied subject's former experience of the situation. Hence, Martinelli (2000) is right when, in contrast with the idea defended by Dilthey that empathy feeds partly on experience and memory, he argues that one cannot always find these resources within oneself. According to him, one can feel empathy for people suffering from hunger or for homeless people without having experienced hunger or without having to experience homelessness. The very notion of 'empathic understanding' as forged by the social sciences, with its association of experience and imagination, following Weber and Dilthey, accounts for this intellectual construction. As Gauss (2003) writes: "In the social sciences, […] empathic understanding refers to our deliberate attempts to identify ourselves with another, accounting for his actions by our own immediate experience of our motivations and attitudes in similar circumstances as we remember or imagine them". Thus, it is no longer as necessary to have lived the same experience as to be able to imagine what we would feel if we were to live it. The Encyclopaedia Britannica (1999 edition) defines empathy as: "the ability to imagine oneself in another's place and understand the other's feelings, desires, ideas and actions" (Vaknin 1999). The experience is therefore not the one that we need to have had prior to the empathic feeling, but the one that actually produces that feeling. This is what emerges from the definition of Ch. Morris (1996: 442, quoted by Vaknin 1999), for whom: "closely related to the ability to read other people's emotions is empathy [...] empathy depends not only on one's ability to identify someone else's emotions but also on one's capacity to put oneself in the other person's place and to experience an appropriate emotional response".

The conceptualization proposed by Barnes & Thagard (1997) for the terms empathy and sympathy enables us to specify the status of the experience in these two situations. For them, empathy "is a more extensive concept than sympathy; it signifies the ability to comprehend another's state without actually experiencing that state". On this point they cite Wispe (1991: 80): "In empathy one acts 'as if' one were the other person… the object of empathy is understanding. The object of sympathy is the other person's well-being. In sum, empathy is a way of knowing; sympathy is a way of relating"[4]. Barnes & Thagard comment on this as follows: "… sympathy is performed with altruistic ends, but empathy may or may not be motivated by good intentions" (p. 708). This distinction is subject to debate because there is no guarantee that the doctor needs to feel sympathy to treat and thus to do good to a patient. What is assumed to characterize sympathy as opposed to empathy is no longer relevant when the concern to do good enters into the definition of a professional activity. The fact that doctors are not required to feel sympathy is attested de facto by many medical professionals. As Martinelli (2000) says, empathy and antipathy can go together.

The distinction between these terms relates partly to the debate relative to the status of experience in the empathic phenomenon. In many studies that

[4] See also Wispe 1987.

set out to define the nature of the difference between the two concepts, the emphasis is on the act of understanding underlying the feeling of empathy. Thus, for Switankowsky (2000: 89), sympathy is "feeling another individual's predicament [...] leading to a type of emotional identification between two individuals. Empathy consists of understanding another person's situation". Yet understanding does not necessarily mean knowledge. As Wispe (1991: 89) points out: "it is a very long journey from understanding to knowing and understanding, while a component of knowledge, cannot be construed as knowledge".

## Empathy and knowledge

In medicine, as in anthropology, empathy may be seen as a tool or a strategy. In fact it is certainly more than that: doctors' own relationship with death, for instance, certainly impacts on their empathic relationship with patients with serious diseases. While the empathic relationship is believed to be useful in establishing a relationship of proximity between the players in many interactions, including between doctors and patients, it is often seen as indispensable in the relationship between observer and observed in anthropology. Most social scientists accept this idea, following Weber and Dilthey who, as we have seen, considered empathy as the very foundation of the method peculiar to the social sciences (on this point see also Bakker 1999). Empathic understanding is a prerequisite to sociological understanding.

Apart from the consensus around this issue in social science, it seems relevant to wonder whether the usefulness of empathy implies its necessity. Or, more precisely, does the empathic relationship have to remain a constant for knowledge to be possible? Although there is no doubt that empathy is a specific characteristic of the anthropological approach, it is also true that the extended periods of field research required in ethnology favour empathy. But even if regular frequentation of the people studied facilitates the establishment of an empathic relationship, the knowledge resulting from the former is not necessarily contingent on the latter. This is probably where the polysemy of the word "understand" (understand the Other) applies most. One can know and frequent someone enough to understand his/her acts (to explain their motives and recognize their meaning) without understanding emotionally and without ever being able to put oneself in that person's place. Consider the following case. During research on the models of interpretation of disease undertaken in Paris and surrounding areas, I studied a family in which the father had kidney failure and was dialysed at home. This family consisted of this man (a tax collector), his wife (a nurse), and their two children, a girl and a boy. The father shared his bed with his daughter and the mother shared hers with her son, and both ardently defended far right-wing ideas. While the fact of frequenting these people enabled me to understand (and to give meaning to) the way in which they perceived and dealt with disease, I do not think that it ever enabled me to "put myself in their place" (regarding either their domestic choices or their political opinions). In this case, empathy was not necessary for the analysis. And despite its utility in understanding the phenomena and subjects studied, it must be followed by an objective view. Putting oneself in someone else's place means trying to have the same point of view on things. If I sit on the chair on which X is seated it will enable me to see what and how he or she sees, but I would have to change chairs to see what his or her place is in the overall game of social relations. It is therefore necessary to leave empathy to attain knowledge.

The possibility that we have of understanding what a person feels in a given situation, that prompts them to act in a particular way, tells us nothing about our perception of that person and our feelings for him or her[5]. The same applies to doctors. Even if a family has a distinct dislike for a doctor, if their child is running a high fever their antipathy will not prevent the doctor from feeling empathy and putting himself in the parents' place, that is, understanding their concern because it reminds him of his own experience (although this will not make him any more capable of dealing with the fever). The ability to understand patients or informants, on an emotional level, can be facilitated if the experience they are having resonates with that of the doctor or ethnologist. On the other hand, unlike the doctor, the ethnologist necessarily has to deploy a huge effort to stand back from his or her own perception of the phenomenon under analysis, in order to avoid the risk of transferring his or her own system of representations onto it.

This is the risk that Becker (1999) took, for instance, when she chose to study the way in which individuals experience the appearance of a disease or a sudden disruption in their lives. A noteworthy feature of her approach is the fact that her personal experience is at the centre of her intellectual inter-

---

[5] While it is true that empathy can hardly be conceived of without its connection to sympathy, this association should not allude to their synonymy nor lead us to conclude that it exists. We can put ourselves in someone's place and understand their thoughts and acts even if we do not like them; conversely, we can experience difficulty in identifying with someone for whom we feel sympathy. As Snow (2000) notes, "there is a difference between feeling an emotion *for* someone, and feeling an emotion *with* someone" (my underlining). The condition of empathy is then the fact of moving closer to what the subject is experiencing or to his/her position in society, rather than to what he/she is.

est in the subject. This study of disturbed, even broken lives results, in a sense, from a reflexive approach. Gay Becker tried to understand how people experience a disruption, in order to deal with the one that she had experienced in her own personal life. She explains to the reader that she spent her childhood in a marginal community, her family being members of what she refers to as "an atypical protestant sect", the Christian Scientists, in which her grandmother was a healer. As a child she never saw doctors nor participated in activities at school, and it was in this context that she developed an allergic pathology and asthma. She believes that what she was experiencing was a situation of "incorporated distress". Her condition and her family's failure to provide her with the possibility of healing caused her to turn to another type of medicine, biomedicine. This constituted a major break with family traditions. Her experience enabled her to be readily received by the anthropological community that tends, she says, to celebrate marginality, and prompted her to choose as a research subject biomedicine, a field that was, in a sense, foreign to her. She explains that she considered herself in a suitable position to take it as a subject of anthropological investigation and that, by contrast, she would have had difficulty studying popular healing systems that were familiar to her – precisely because she felt she was too close to be able to study them "without passion". I can only approve of a choice made out of a concern to preserve the precious distance from the object of anthropological study; on the other hand, I cannot entirely subscribe to her reflexive analysis when she affirms that, not having been "socialized" in the context of biomedicine, at least before adulthood, she did not consider it with the same emotional charge as Christian Scientism. We can legitimately reply that the fact of belonging to a marginal group like the Christian Scientists is hardly likely to make her view biomedicine in a neutral way, without passion! Finally, of the different events likely to disrupt a person's existence, Gay Becker focused in particular on the subject of "sterility", also inspired by her own personal experience for several years. Even if the subjectivity of her approach (attested by her interest in problems that marked her personal experience) does not reduce the acuity of her analysis, I wonder to what extent the empathy that she felt for her asthmatic or sterile informants was productive, and whether she did not superimpose her own representations on those of the individuals studied.

## To conclude

The different studies mentioned above were chosen to contribute to reflection on the role of empathy in the knowledge production process. I hoped in this way to establish whether empathy produces knowledge and whether knowledge production requires empathy or the sharing of an experience.

Although the aim of medical activity is generally to heal, whereas that of ethnological study is only to analyse, the question relative to the doctor's and the ethnologist's respective positions regarding the subjects treated or studied, and regarding the role of empathy in the knowledge process, enables us to distinguish the necessity of empathy in these two types of relationship. While the doctor's empathy can be seen as an asset (and not as a sufficient condition to constitute his or her competence, as opposed to the lay representations mentioned above, borrowed from different cultural contexts), the ethnologist's empathy is probably far more problematical. Although ethnologists have to observe and share their subject's experience very closely, and although this affords them a more immediate grasp of the subject, they must also be able to understand another individual, different to the first one, who does not experience things in the same way.

If we examine these diverse research situations we clearly see that understanding has to leave the emotional field if it is to be truly intellectual. The ethnologist's empathy can then contribute to the knowledge process provided that he or she is able, at some point, to move away from it. Perhaps the ethnologist should assume the loser's role in the game of musical chairs; he or she should be able to change places constantly, to sit on different chairs, except on his or her own chair that has been removed. And if he or she is left without a chair, it is precisely to avoid the place of an individual engaged in this play of social relations. This is what will finally enable him or her to be excluded from the game and therefore to analyse it better. To sum up, whereas medical empathy may appear as purely beneficial, the ethnologist's empathy is beneficial for a while only. Although it opens doors that possibly remain closed to other disciplines, it is something that has to be jettisoned at some point in the process.

All these examples highlight the ambiguity that can exist when empathy is conceived of by representing the Other (the one with whom the empathic relationship is realized) as a monolithic entity. In fact, prevailing discourse on the ethnologist's need to develop an empathic relationship with his or her informants contains the implicit idea that informants are an homogeneous whole, occupying a single place only, in which the ethnologist can put him-

or herself to feel what this Other (conceived of in the singular and thus from a simplified point of view) might experience. But informants have different experiences and social positions, and are engaged in different power struggles, so that it is impossible to develop empathy with all of them. This is a reality that reflection on empathy generally seems to overlook.

This distancing is necessary if empathy is not to produce an over-simplified view of the object. When the ethnologist puts him- or herself in an informant's place, it enables him or her to see what the informant sees. However, it is then necessary to leave that place in order to see the informant and to see how others see him or her. A way of avoiding this situation of reductive empathy is perhaps dual or even multiple empathy, facilitated by an understanding of the different protagonists in a social relationship. For instance, anyone who wants to study the issue of information and the role of lies in the doctor-patient relationship (a subject on which I am currently working), has to try to put him- or herself "in the place" of both doctors and patients. Feeling empathy for only one party in this relationship would involve the risk of obtaining biased knowledge on the issue of information.

In medicine the distancing is obtained immediately via objects – measuring instruments, tensiometer, stethoscope, radiography, blood tests, clinical examination –, all of which enable the subject to remain in the position of an object. In contrast, anthropologists have to make an effort to extract themselves from that place, to reverse the point of view. Empathy then naturally produces knowledge. While doctors do not necessarily need detachment since it will not change their analysis of the situation, for ethnologists the break with empathy is essential to obtain critical knowledge. After savouring its benefits in terms of data collection, they have to give up empathy before analysing that information.

Finally, a fundamental difference lies in the very nature of the relationship in which empathy is felt. The medical relationship is in fact dual: it involves the doctor and the patient, and the knowledge produced by the former is intended for the latter. In contrast, the ethnological relationship is ternary: it involves the ethnologist, the informants, and the public in general (readers, society) for which the knowledge is produced. In other words, in one instance empathy serves the patient; in the other, it serves the public. Not only is the purpose not the same; the actual use of empathy has a different function in the process of knowledge production. We see here the cognitive and therefore heuristic virtue of empathy, provided it can be controlled. Because it can be useful, even necessary, in the research process, but also because it has to be discarded in the knowledge project, empathy in ethnology is perhaps both the condition and the illusion of knowledge.

## References

Bakker, H.

1999 Wilhelm Dilthey: Classical sociological theorist. *Quarterly Journal of Ideology* 22, 1&2: 43-82.

Barnes, A. & Thagard, P.

1997 Empathy and analogy. *Dialogue: Canadian Philosophical Review* 36: 705-720.

Becker, G.

1999 *Disrupted lives. How people create meaning in a chaotic world.* Berkeley, Los Angeles, London: University of California Press.

Dilthey, W.

1959 The understanding of other persons and their life-expressions. Tr. J.J. Kuehl. In: P. Gardiner (ed.) *Theories of history: Readings in classical and contemporary sources*. New York: Free Press. [From Gesammelte Schriften Volume VII: 205-220.] pp. 213-225.

Fainzang, S.

1986 *"L'intérieur des choses". Maladie, divination et reproduction sociale chez les Bisa du Burkina.* Paris: L'Harmattan (Préface de M. Augé).

1996 *Ethnologie des anciens alcooliques. La liberté ou la mort.* Paris: Presses Universitaires de France (Collection: Ethnologies).

2001 *Médicaments et société. Le patient, le médecin et l'ordonnance.* Paris: Presses Universitaires de France.

Fainzang, S. & Journet, O.

1988 *La femme de mon mari. Ethnologie du mariage polygamique en Afrique et en France*. Paris: L'Harmattan.

Gauss, Ch. E.

2003 Empathy. *Dictionary of the history of ideas*. The Electronic Text Center, University of Virginia Library. Charlottesville: The Gale Group. [http://etext.lib.virginia.edu/DicHist/dict.html].

Haynes, R.B.; Taylor, D. & Sackett, D.L. (eds.)

1979 *Compliance in health care*. Baltimore: John Hopkins University Press.

Morris, Ch.

1996 *Psychology. An introduction*. (9th edition) Prentice Hall.

Martinelli, B.

2000 *L'empathie en ethnologie*. Introductory paper to the Idemec/MMSH Seminar on Empathy (Aix-en-Provence, April 7, 2000).

Snow, N.E.

2000 Empathy. *American Philosophical Quarterly* 37, 1: 65-78.

Spiro, H.; Peschel, E.; McCrea Curnen, M.G. & St. James, D. (eds.)

1993 *Empathy and the practice of medicine: Beyond pills and the scalpel*. New Haven, London: Yale University Press.

Stein, H.F.

1980 Medical anthropology and Western medicine. *The Journal of Psychological Anthropology* 3/2: 185-205.

Switankowsky, I.

2000 Sympathy and empathy. *Philosophy Today* 44, 1: 86-92.

Vaknin, S.
1999 *On empathy* [http://samvak.tripod.com/empathy.html].

Weber, M.
1971 *Economie et société*. Paris: Plon.

Wispe, L.
1987 History of the concept of empathy. In: N. Eisenberg & J. Strayer (eds.) *Empathy and its development.* Cambridge: Cambridge University Press, pp. 17-37.

Wispe L.
1991 *The psychology of sympathy*. New York: Plenum Press.

# The Other's pain is the anthropologist's strain. Crisis of proximity in medical anthropology of suffering

Els van Dongen

Participant-observation is a much debated but little explained method that is important in anthropology. The paradox of participant-observation – proximity and distance – seems to speak louder in medical anthropology today than it ever has. Anthropologists take different positions. Some argue that distance is a necessary prerequisite for "objectivity" and rational knowledge production (see Fainzang, this volume). Others have argued that involvement and proximity – linked to moral responsibility – should be stressed because anthropology is a relational science or has to be applied and participatory. Some even argue for a militant anthropology (Scheper-Hughes 1995). In this paper, I do not elaborate on the debates about the nature of anthropology and ethics in anthropological fieldwork. Rather, I argue that the proximity of anthropologists to their research participants or informants has become problematic, as has the traditional practice of doing fieldwork and building relationships.

The situation in the field has changed. Violence and post-violence situations make some fieldwork problematic, if not impossible. The needs and interests of people openly contradict those of the anthropologist; human suffering and misery are incomprehensible. This brought to the fore the issue of proximity to research participants and its effects on the body of medical anthropological knowledge. Because anthropology's method is intrinsically linked to its theoretical orientations, structural and everyday violence not only has ramifications for fieldwork and thus for the depth of data, but also for its interpretation and theoretical orientation. When it is difficult to grasp the intensity and depth of human suffering, it is certainly difficult to describe and explain it. Ethical alibis may lead to bias: With whom is an anthropologist proximate? With whom are they not close and for what reasons? And if an anthropologist is near to certain persons, can he or she also be proximate with others? I explore some of those effects and questions and illustrate my arguments with examples of my own work and that of my students in South Africa.

Anthropology has become a discipline that brings grievances and suffering to public attention by describing local worlds of suffering and misery and by means of an alternating pair in fieldwork – distance and proximity. Together with a long-standing relationship, this pair is thought to be necessary for obtaining an intersubjective understanding of the Other and ourselves. Ethnographies often express a strong personal commitment. "Interpersonal experience" is a concept that points to shared human conditions such as loss, mourning or pain (Kleinman 1995). Counter transference, originally a psychoanalytic concept, is used to describe and analyse the positive and negative effects of proximity (Tobin 1986). However, we must question if anthropologists can imagine and understand what is at stake for people under conditions of poverty, oppression or violence when social distance is far and close relationships are difficult to establish.

Anthropology struggles with the nature of relations. Since the birth of anthropological fieldwork, an important method – participant observation – has been under the scrutiny of anthropologists themselves as well as criticised by others. From the start, Malinowski's groundbreaking work begged two important questions: How to put theory into fieldwork and how could an anthropologist grasp the insider's point of view? Merleau-Ponty's (1973) statement that the Other is always on the margin of what we see and hear is perhaps also true for the anthropologist's relationships with the Other. One may have so much noise in one's head that it is not possible to hear the Other. Theories, positions, interests but also (over)involvement may stand in the way of hearing the Other. The Other's silence, which is so frustrating to anthropologists who are focused on verbal accounts of their informants, has perhaps an unforeseen dimension. De Swaan (1982: 142, my translation) states: "When one does not want to speak, others obviously cannot listen…"

Anthropology's most precious and valued method – fieldwork – has been under siege; there have been crises after crises in the discipline. First, anthropology suffered from a crisis of interpretation and representation. The "old" ideology of transparency, representation and immediacy of experience was seriously questioned, and it was recognised that ethnographic truths were inherently partial. Fabian's work (1983) clearly shows how anthropologists create their objects, and his argument for coevalness marks in my view the start of a democratic anthropological fieldwork that acknowledges and respects human rights. Coevalness demands a somewhat different relationship between anthropologists and informants; it demands "speaking with" instead of "speaking about". When people are in deep suffering, this "speaking with" is under siege, because, as Marguerite Duras in La Douleur argues: "The only answer one can give to this crime is to make it a crime of all of us. To share. Just as the idea of equality, brotherhood. To be able to bear it, to endure the thought, to share the crime." (Duras 1985, my translation).

So, we can ask if the anthropologist should share suffering and responsibility for what happens to people in war zones, postcolonial areas or in social suffering. This is not unproblematic, as we will see.

The crisis of interpretation and representation was followed by another crisis: that of relevance. Two important arguments were made. The first was that the uniqueness of the anthropological method was not reserved for anthropology, since other disciplines, such as journalism or visual sciences could do "the job as good as anthropology", only faster and cheaper. Although media may dramatise suffering and the consequences of violence, they are not based on (long-standing) social relationships and intersubjectivity and do not possess the same objectives as anthropology.

The second argument was that the traditional practice of fieldwork and writing an interpretative account based on ethnographic insights had become untenable, because societies were no longer bounded centres and the unit of anthropological research does not approximate the realities people have to live in. In the context of suffering and violence, I disagree with the argument that media do similar jobs as anthropologists. I agree that anthropologists have to work in less well-demarcated areas, war-stricken zones, diasporas and fragmented communities. But to me it seems more a challenge than a crisis.

There is third crisis: a crisis of participation and relationality. It seems that anthropologists have increasingly become "passers-by". In many regions, it has become almost impossible to participate in the daily lives of their research participants, because of practical reasons, moral or ethical arguments or danger. There will be less opportunity to develop the intimate relationships and trust that characterise proximity, which is often needed for discussing sensitive issues such as experiences of violence and more in general human suffering. This – in turn – could mean that the alternating of distance and proximity, which is thought to be so important for anthropological study, is more or less disturbed.

The question that arises from these (experienced) crises in anthropology is this: What will be the consequences for anthropology, for its relevance and for its theory of suffering? In the remaining part of my paper, I will answer this question. I will start with the crisis of participation. I will then elaborate on relevance and representation. In my conclusions I will discuss the consequences for anthropology and its theory of suffering.

## Proximity in crisis

The traditional practice of fieldwork and the common dynamics of proximity became untenable for several reasons. In particular, when anthropologists work in conflict areas and focus on human suffering, relationality is difficult to establish. Fieldwork has become fragmented, partial and more an office job in the sense of occurring on a time schedule than ever. This is not only caused by financial constraints or obligations the anthropologist may have elsewhere. The reasons are manifold. In their book *Fieldwork under fire* Nordstrom & Robben (1995) brought together papers that discuss the constraints and research problems for anthropologists who study violence. They mention the dangers (physical, social and mental), existential shocks, anxiety, chaos, suspicion, ethical and moral dilemmas, and more. The authors also discuss the theoretical and methodological consequences of doing fieldwork in conflict or post-conflict areas.

The situations anthropologists often encounter require a change in methodology. It is not suggested that they refrain from ethnographical work because of ethical reasons, or the risk of secondary traumatisation or physical threat, or because of powerlessness vis-à-vis incomprehensible misery and suffering. The authors mention, for example, "accidental anthropology" meaning that a researcher should not stick to the research plan at all costs but be willing to make use of unexpected events. They mention making dangers in fieldwork into a methodological issue and not to avoid them. After reading through this volume, my main conclusion is that although the authors maintain that fieldwork can make an important contribution to the study and understanding of violence and suffering, it needs a thorough rethinking, not only for the anthropologist personally but also in the education of anthropologists.

A main issue to be discussed is the proximity-in-crisis. To speak with Taussig, violence is slippery and seems to escape the academic and scholarly approach. It has contradictions of laughter and suffering, of fear and hope, of absurdity and commonplace (Taussig 1987). It has perpetrators, victims, collaborators and bystanders. These contradictions and differences shake the anthropologist's moral grounds and may constrain relationality in the field. Silence and lies deceive and lead one anthropologist to conclude "that the many directions I had been sent to were only intended to entice me away from where I was already standing" (Robben 1995: 99). It is a painful awareness that informants have become agents and editors of the anthropological encounter and the ethnography. They have intentions, needs and interests and may therefore manipulate the research.

Politics of forgetting can draw the anthropologist into processes of world making that blur deep internal conflicts and make her feel manipulated. This was certainly the case in South Africa, Western Cape Province, where I did my fieldwork. South Africa was described in media and research as having a culture of violence resulting from the Apartheid era and colonialism. Research and efforts of the government and non-governmental organisations were focused on the issues of violence. Recent forms of violence such as gangsterism, sexual violence or domestic violence, were explained as consequences of past political upheaval, oppression, poverty and economic manipulation. South Africa offers a sad history of what Crais (2002) has called "the politics of evil". Without going into the historical details, one may say that this politics of evil has left South Africans in deeply rooted frustration, hatred, envy and conflict. Not that these qualms are directly observable or visible, on the contrary: Nobody wanted to be nasty about the New South Africa; everyone seemed to be full of hope and goodwill; loyalty to the great historical moment was without doubt.

When I first entered my field as a stranger I was impressed by the enthusiasm, the openness and optimism. Although the seduction of becoming involved actively in "world making" and happy optimism was strong, I felt restrictions because I soon "sensed" an underlying drama about destroyed social and cultural structures. Walking through the streets with informants and listening to their comments and gossip about their neighbours and fellow citizens, I became aware that the consequences of the past gnawed at the rainbow nation and even at my relationships with people in my fieldwork among elderly in the townships on the Cape Flats and on the farms in the Western Cape Province of South Africa. The elderly were frustrated with the new system, but in their stories contradictions emerged. They told about apartheid as a time of "law and order" but they also said that this time was terrible. Notably, their lament was not about poverty or oppression. Their main frustration was that they were not free to go where they wanted. "The time of the passes" still caused them deep pain, just as their relationships with their children do in the present. The two recurrent themes in the stories of the elderly were related and needed an explanation, but could hardly be discussed. The culture of silence (or was it secrecy?) triggered proximity and coevalness. In fact, my belief in Fabian's description of fieldwork as a coeval activity (Fabian 1983) was fiercely attacked.

Compared to the Malinowskian method of fieldwork (full time residence for several years), my method seemed very meagre to me. Practical reasons such as lecturing at my university, lack of finances, a sudden illness or engagement in other projects fragmented my fieldwork into short periods, so that I could only work on rapport with the elderly, their caregivers or family any time I was able to spend a couple of weeks in South Africa. It could happen that people died during my absence, or had moved. A more serious consequence of this fragmentation was that explanations and interpretations of data were difficult to make because part of the knowledge of the social context simply could not be retrieved. I felt hindered by my style of fieldwork.

Another issue was that I felt like I had an "office job", working with the elderly from eight in the morning until five in the afternoon (my South African students did the same). I could not live in the townships with the elderly with whom I did research because at that time, I would have not only endangered myself, but also my hosts. On the farms, meeting the elderly in the evening was impossible, because my hosts had simply forbidden me to go outside at that time, because of the drunkenness of the men, especially during weekends. In such a situation proximity but also distance became difficult. I felt forced into a distancing culture of fear that makes people looking over their shoulders and made them deeply distrustful toward each other. How would I be able to understand the suffering of the elderly who fled to the old age centres during the day and had to endure the harshness of their kin and others during the nights when distrust had become a basic condition? Moreover, it was a distrust fed by hard feelings of the past.

Violence had become mundane in the lives of elderly and others. On Saturday nights they heard the shootings of the gangs; they could point out the no-go areas in their neighbourhoods; they told harrowing stories of abuse and abandonment. Older people withdrew into their rooms when family members were quarrelling or when their kin came home. I had to reconsider common concepts of the pathological/abnormal withdrawal. For me such events were abnormal, for them it seems to have become normal and the best thing to do. Extreme withdrawal of older people would probably be labelled in the Netherlands as pathological; here it was a strategy to survive.

Moral dilemmas had a deep impact on my relationships in South Africa. My main research topic is social memory. But memories of older persons were not the main concern for them (Van Dongen 2005b). Urgent questions arose for me: How could I study memory without talking about the past? Why is it that people in western or westernised countries have such a great interest, maybe even an obsession, with memory? I am not sure of the answers. Part of the explanation could be that our future has been lost and that we believe that we can plan and control our lives. Moreover, our paradigms of memory and remembrance include an optimistic perspective on healing aspects of remembrance. It is often argued that remembering has a therapeutic dimension (Das et al. 2001, Soyinka 1999). In the case of older persons, for example, it is believed that reminiscence in later life enables the establishment of continuity and reconciliation. However, although "giving voice to older persons" lives' (Ferreira & Van Dongen 2004) may express (positive) proximity and involvement in their lives, it can also mean, as Spivak (1988) argues, that by speaking out and claiming a cultural identity, the subaltern will re-inscribe their subordinate position in society. This would mean an ethnocentric extension of the western academic logos. That would make me cautious and careful, at the same time putting me at greater distance. How could I account for the heterogeneity of the older persons and build a proximate relationship? Furthermore, "doing memory" caused older persons sometimes much pain.

Last (2000) counts researchers among the watchers of, for example, violence. He shows that the European obsession with the past may largely differ from what people in Africa perceive as relevant. This means that we will have to understand the role of the interpreters, in this case the anthropologists. There is always the danger that an anthropologist refrains in "little better than postcolonial discourse". For example, as a white, European, academic person I was a western and historical product. For some people, "anthropologist" sounds very much like "colonialist" and they would ask me the uneasy questions to which I never found an answer: "What gives you the right to come here and ask all your questions? You will take my answers home and earn your money; what good is in it for us?" Such awareness and questions from the elderly and the members of their social networks can easily be explained by the poverty most of my informants have to live in. While poverty is an important part of the explanation, it is not all of it.

The unmistakable commodification of old people that has taken place during the last ten years had made people suspicious and sometimes even hostile to my questions. Others commodify their stories, their cultural knowledge and position as pensioners (for example audio taping life stories and sell them to interested organisations, or withdrawing cultural knowledge about handicrafts and utensils for selling without any benefit for the elderly, or claiming pension money for living or drinking). These two factors – my position as watcher or maybe bystander or even as assessor and the frequent commodification of cultural knowledge, made proximity to the elderly difficult to establish. Even when it seemed that we related very well, my suspicion was fed by this knowledge and made me often doubt the value of the data of my fieldwork. Suspicion by informants, however, but also of anthropologists must be questioned and used, since it may lead to a critical stance of both, which in turn will disable dialogue and participation of local people. As Spivak (1988) argues, granting collective speech to the subaltern has a logocentric assumption of cultural solidarity among a heterogeneous people, and a dependence upon western intellectuals to speak for the subaltern.

The anthropologist's role that is put upon her may lead to thin descriptions, which may result in over-stressing the suffering of victims and blindness to the suffering of their children. The result is over-simplification and incompleteness of local situations.

According to Scheper-Hughes & Bourgois (2004) anthropologists have the duty to make their own political views known and to contribute to human liberation. This role as "shock trooper" and "alarmist" and militant anthropology has downfalls. If the anthropologist and anthropology are obliged morally to provide data for social change, the science looses its credibility, because research is influenced by a self-imposed political agenda and data will be useless for the scientific field. "… if ethnography itself is nothing more than methodology for political advocacy, then why should we trust the data it puts forth any more than we trust the heavily biased data produced by partisan policy research institutes (...) that seek to advance platforms instead of build knowledge" (Kovats-Bernat 2002: 219).

Building proximity became also extremely difficult in cases of intra-group conflicts filled with envy, hatred and resentment. When a society must face interracial relationships, which can represent relationships between perpetrators and victims, unequal social and economic structures and inheritance of violence, intra-group relations are not easily and openly discussed. One has to make new identities as a group. To me this is one of the most difficult parts of an ethnographic study, because moral considerations, painful memories of deep suffering and danger of disturbance of a fragile equilibrium that people have created in their lives would lie in wait.

To clarify this gap between the anthropological perspectives on the one hand and incomprehensible pain and suffering on the other hand, I will use an example. My intent was to gain an understanding of the lives of those who had outlived wars, conflicts, apartheid, poverty and the atrocities they all entail. As I wrote before, it was difficult to talk with the elderly about their lives; they were willing to share memories, but only in a certain way. We know that memory is vulnerable to manipulation and interests of the tellers;

we know that we will have to search for facts and sift truth from fiction and misinformation. We have developed methods and perspectives to do so. But do we know how to deal with the intense pain, secrets and shame and to explain and translate it in an anthropological manner that can be used in other contexts and be supportive in post conflict situations?

I discovered that Xhosa and coloured elderly in particular shared their memories about the past not just to recount the past but to show younger generations how the past was a much better time. It seemed paradoxical that stories about violence and atrocities they had to endure in their work, their marriage and their youth would bespeak of better days. What I saw as pathological human conditions had become a normal part of the elderly's entire lives. Such knowledge should have consequences for anthropological explanations and also for support programmes. In the case of the latter I see a problem: what will openness about the past achieve in such cases?

It has become clear that silence and forgetting is a much-used strategy to deal with atrocities of the past. Shame and guilt play an important role. If I had perceived the elderly only as victims and had denied their agency, I would have never come across this secret and painful problem. Although much has been written about elderly abuse in South Africa and the abandonment of elderly, even about a social form of gerontocide (Van Dongen 2005a), little has been written about the elderly's rude abandonment of their children and grandchildren and about their contempt towards younger generations. Their memories were not remembrance in the sense of re-connecting people across generations and history, but rather harsh moral statements about the present, which eventually would differentiate them from the rest of the group.

I met a culture of the silenced when I tried to find out what the reasons for such rude condemnation of others in their social and racial group were. Most of the elderly of my research had adopted a strategy of survival: silence, submissiveness and surrender, which were precisely at the core of the intra-group conflicts. The younger generations – the children of the elderly who fought the freedom struggle and their childrens' children strongly rebelled against the elderly's submissiveness, compromises with whites and surrender to their situation in the apartheid era and thereafter. The fact that many elderly had left their children behind when they migrated to the city to look for jobs further compounded this. Intergenerational relationships are usually characterised by reciprocity (see for example Holmes Rhodes & Holmes 1995: 116-120), which means that when a parent invests in the children, the children are more likely to invest in their parents when they have become old. Through processes out of the hands of the elderly such as poverty, but certainly also through intra-group tensions and resentment, this process of reciprocity was disturbed. The elderly's children and their children's children told me this (in a hesitating way), but the elderly could not. I could not discuss this issue with them, because abandoning kin and going to live in an old age home was a shameful thing, which one does not do in a culture where the ethos of *ubuntu*, ultimate sharing among one's own social group, is so deeply inscribed into people's bodies and minds. (*Ubuntu* is still practiced by the elderly, e.g. when they care for orphans and kin that the AIDS pandemic has left behind.) While the elderly were abused, exploited, raped and ignored as a consequence of the past, their social group stresses their wisdom and dignity. Keeping up appearances is important. My title – mama (an often used title for older women who deserve respect in a society) – became symbolic of the anthropologist's crisis of proximity: unable to discuss this painful experience of shame and suffering, put into a position of a white woman with whom the elderly could interact in a way they were used to when they still worked, forcing me to remain at a distance when it came to social secrets. What would it mean to open a well of pain and conflict in a time that is not ripe for such an endeavour?

I struggled to find a balance between proximity and distance. Sometimes I felt so involved in the elderly's lives and their stories that I lost the will and courage to analyse and interpret them. Sometimes I was too absorbed by the theoretical noise and the labyrinth of theories about social memory that I lost my connection to the local world of suffering. The words of Scheper-Hughes & Bourgois (2004: 26) come into mind:

"Those for whom the representation of hunger, misery, and violence is central to their life's work need to continually resensitize their audience as well as themselves to the state of emergency in which we live. To do so we must locate proper distance from our subjects. Not so distant as to objectify their suffering, and not so close that we turn the sufferer into an object of pity, contempt or public spectacle. We need to avoid anaesthetization of misery as much as a descent into political rhetorics and polemics."

Another constraint in establishing a close relationship was my role as mediator that many forced upon me. I was seen as a mediator between the haves and the have-nots. Their needs were often so urgent and their suffering was so beyond my comprehension that I often thought of becoming a fundraiser instead of a researcher. Not that the elderly and others thought that research was unimportant, but they had a very particular idea about it that was different from mine. It seemed that the elderly, especially in old age homes, were so accustomed to researchers who literally popped into their space and did their interviews and then went off, that they often started our conversations with: "What are your questions?" With this question they created a distance that needed hard work to overcome. One old age centre closed its doors for researchers, because as they said: they did not receive any benefits from their research. The close relationships I did establish with the elderly could easily become disrupted. When those relationships became reciprocal, such as if I gave little gifts or some service or even supported a small project, the envy of others would turn against the person or the group of receivers. I had to navigate the waters of relationality, so to speak, looking carefully for obstacles such as irritation, envy, jealousy, not that would be turned on me, but on my research partner, the older person.

There were numerous other mundane and not so mundane issues that triggered proximity. The places where I worked were places of danger and laughter, of anxiety and immense suffering as well as pleasure. Such contradictions are difficult to grasp. The anger of John, who became aggressive during our conversation and shouted that he had worked his entire life for nothing, has lost everything and now has to be in a wheelchair in an old age home made me ask myself if I should speak with the elderly about their lives if so much pain came to the surface. But the same John would call me and ask me to sit with him at the front door to tell jokes and to listen to the stories of his life. The laughs and often-good moods of people who told me about the terrible atrocities they had to endure just a couple of minutes before puzzled me and were difficult to explain. It reminded me of my work in a mental hospital where such paradoxical and contradictive behaviour alternated with dazzling speed. I did not find adequate explanations for it, but if there is a family resemblance between the two, it may be that the chronicity of suffering made it so mundane that explaining it by traumatisation is insufficient and inadequate. The elderly were not traumatised; they lived a common life. The terrible stories of the elderly can become quite common too for an anthropologist. We may become deaf and forget to search beyond what is said. But searching beyond the said may – in turn – disturb proximity and relationships.

## Anthropology, proximity and theory of suffering

This paper reveals some of the difficulties of modern medical anthropology fieldwork. This fieldwork seems to have become partial and is probably more a jigsaw puzzle than a straightforward path to understanding. We can never be sure when to be proximate and when to distance ourselves. Proximity, it seems, is constrained by moral distrust, the result of a historical process in which "the global village" has been involved and still is.

I wanted to question the oft-heard claim that medical anthropology contributes to a better understanding of human suffering because the anthropologist captures the native point of view, because they participate in the lives of their informants. Beyond this claim lies a Malinowskian belief that the common humanity of all people can be revealed. I read a passage from Malinowski's diary (1989 [1917]: 119): "What is the deepest essence of my investigations? To discover what his (human's) main passions, the motives for his conduct, his aims ... His essential, deepest way of thinking…". My fieldwork and that of others challenges this engagement. I doubt if the deepest way of thinking is similar across societies and cultures. The "natives" can speak for themselves as Frankenberg (1995) already pointed out; our concepts for explaining and describing the paradoxical, even contradictive ways of suffering are still not well developed. We have to deal with silence, day and night, stories, and secrets that cannot be revealed without causing pain and conflict. Sometimes this results in the acknowledgement that suffering may be "beyond human understanding". In others it has caused a switch to a radical medical anthropology or to the use of human rights in their work. Others have refrained from the debate or used a "hit and run" method of interviewing, which is not combined with participatory research and thus is hampered by thresholds to proximity that is necessary for understanding and talking about very sensitive and painful issues; thorough contextualisation of stories is not possible.

All these approaches certainly have value, but I also see some dangers. The example of the secret between elderly and youngsters (see above), but also the relationship between perpetrators, bystanders and victims who have to build a new society together are issues difficult to explain and deal with, especially when medical anthropology limits itself to certain groups, mostly victims. It would gnaw at the core of much medical anthropological work, if we would broaden our scope to perpetrators, whose suffering cannot easily be comprehended. Ethical and moral alibis may lead to withdrawal, so that a comprehensive picture of daily reality and the suffering of all who were involved in atrocities cannot be obtained. The Other's pain is the anthropologist's strain!

Medical anthropology is changing. Applied, participatory research is often seen as the most important way of research. Students express their wish to be educated in such a way that they can immediately apply their skills and knowledge to the pressing issues and suffering in their societies. I met many South African students of medical anthropology who had a deep engagement with suffering and injustice. But, as Moore (1995) already remarked, anthropologists from Asian and African countries have other struggles. They try to transcend the western way of defining and reasoning and to establish other frameworks that are often explicitly linked to political projects of liberation and identity formation. That they develop other ways to obtain their data and develop their knowledge is part of this process. Such cases show that suffering is not only the result of natural evil; it is attributable to the quality of the relationships between humans (Sturm 1998: 162). Besides, an important issue for many people is not how to suffer meaningfully or to interpersonally experience human conditions such as bereavement, loss or oppression. A main issue is how to deal with fate and misfortune (Reynolds Whyte 2005: 246). What kind of medical anthropology is to be developed then? Would it have to be anthropology of relationality? And how do we define proximity? Would it have to be intimately connected with social action, fuelled by critical doubt and for the sake of understanding broadening relationships with different interest groups? Or with ethics and justice? Or is proximity connected to morality and responsibility? Listening to the many ways people suffer, to the historical location of joy and pain, and the many terrors it has unleashed, will matter somehow.

In his Tanner lectures *Experience and its moral modes* in 1998, Kleinman speaks about the "dangerous burden of social suffering". He examines one type of danger: the sources, forms and consequences of social suffering. Kleinman sees suffering as distracting and disquieting, and social suffering as "a marker of disadvantage, relative powerlessness and devastating effects of social change" and in that sense "a moral indicator of cultural or societal disorder" (1998: 391). He argues that compassion and respect nowadays is expressed in terms of human rights and that there is a widening gap between the witnessing of disaster and the feeling of an obligation. Kleinman believes that ethnography is an interpersonal engagement in local moral worlds; a practice of sustaining empathy and engagement; a moral process of engaged listening and commitment to witnessing and to take into account what is at stake for people. This could change sensibility and would contribute to address social suffering. I would like to wholeheartedly agree, but a critic on post-modernistic ethnography comes to my mind, formulated by Wenger (1994: 68): "This does not empower the weak at the expense of the strong; rather, it establishes the rule of the strong by other means." Here, I want to argue that empathically listening to the Other, to be involved in local moral worlds or to commit oneself to witnessing has unexpected effects that may be futile, if those activities do not have consequences. The "dangers of suffering", however, demand more than bringing people's grievances and pain to public attention; they demand "an anthropology of consequence", a pragmatic approach that directs "attention to what people should care about" (Reynolds Whyte 2003). In her inaugural lecture, Reynolds Whyte describes such anthropology as "applying anthropological theory and method to concrete problems in order to change practice." She defines problems as uncertainties, doubts, difficulties and ambiguities. They will have to be followed by action. Plans of action should be chosen with an eye on the consequences, not only on the short term but also on long term ones, reckoning with fallibility. Reynolds Whyte has a point when she argues that anthropology of consequence needs collaboration and critical discussion among scholars of various disciplines. Such an anthropology implies obligation – the need to do something. I want to take this issue a step further and use the concept of responsibility.

Ethnographers may become entangled in the politics (of power, of forgetting, of positioning, etc.) that lie beyond their and their informants' scope and control, but nevertheless these will have a deep impact on their relationship, involvement and proximity. Local moral worlds – of informants and anthropologist – are at stake and may differ or even clash. Informants often refer to the responsibility of others. In my research this responsibility was twofold: as a mediator between informants and policy makers or fund givers on the one hand, and, on the other, the responsibility for historical processes. There is no need to argue that the latter is the most dramatic and the most difficult responsibility an anthropologist can have. Can an anthropologist be responsible for the suffering caused by violence, war and other atrocities?

New meanings change the past. Making a world after violence and amidst violence is public dynamics and the anthropologist is part of this dynamics. But in what dynamics is the anthropologist involved? Arendt (1969) is careful to distinguish power from violence. She reserves power to designate the ability to act in concert. It emerges from deliberation and association and is a result of consultation in a public forum. People-in-power are empowered by a supportive group. Alternatively, power implies collaboration between self and other. For anthropologists, this would mean that informants and anthropologists collaborate. However, I believe this is a "false" collaboration as long as researchers (and others) work with the idea that people's suffering can be relieved by empowerment and association without recognising the past. To show that social memory is a dynamic process, it is necessary to surround the stories with social, economic and political contexts, not to test the truth, but to show the dynamics. "One of the fundamental features of anthropology is the view that cultural values are historic products and, therefore, that one should not ethnocentrically assume that the values of one's society are more legitimate, superior, or universal than those of other people" (Hinton 2002: 2). However, the consequences of such a relativistic point of view can paralyse intervention and an anthropology of consequence. It easily ends as moral equivalence (Cushman 2004: 11) and the statement that all parties are guilty. Relativism also results in anthropological knowledge being used to legitimise extremism. Cushman goes as far as to state that he argues for verisimilitude, the application of universal cultural truths. I argue that a relativistic standpoint for the local worlds of truth and morality is the only way to try to understand people's realities.

Violence, in Arendt's perspective, is an employment of a technique, an instrument of force and a matter of imposition. Informants often experience this imposition, and it is incompatible with power. Arendt argues that violence is a reaction to political frustration and emerges from the obstruction that denies people participation in public processes. Her perspective makes clear that the presence of an anthropologist can invoke this frustration. It constraints proximity; it demands an answer, which goes beyond dramatising violence and social suffering. Suffering needs an operative moral philosophy (Wolfe 1989). Although several anthropologists have studied and written about human suffering (Bourdieu 1993, Das et al. 2001, Davis 1992), we still need to study the different modes of expressions, conceptualisations, symbols, causes, explanations and endurance of it. Medical anthropology should not limit itself to illness.

Anthropologists and informants are moral beings. Responsibility, which I use in the sense that responsibility means being able to make good moral and practical judgements, needs collaborative thinking and reflection on consequences of anthropological work, but it also needs moral confidence. The crisis in fieldwork and proximity shows that this moral confidence in each other has to be re-evaluated. I am not suggesting that this is easy. Moral practices are fundamentally complex and non-integrated and describing them is not a morally neutral act (Moody-Adams 1997). To share suffering, to take responsibility, and to make suffering bearable is not the same as "taking the suffering away". Responsibility also means that we will have to look for collaboration with others (informants, colleagues) in which we try to find similarities in our moral worlds, because to be understood and to understand, a minimum of shared morality is necessary. Anthropological research, characterised by proximity and responsibility, shows us that in post-war societies, there is often no place for personal stories. There is a "moral quarantine", which makes it impossible to describe what happened and is happening.

**References**

Ahmed, A. & Shore, C. (eds.)

1995 *The future of anthropology. Its relevance to the contemporary world.* London: Athlone.

Arendt, H.

1969 *On violence*. New York: Harcourt Brace.

Bourdieu, P. (ed.)

1993 *La misère du monde*. Paris: Seuil.

Crais, C.

2002 *The politics of evil. Magic, state, and the political imagination in South Africa*. Cambridge: Cambridge University Press.

Cushman, T.

2004 Anthropology and genocide in the Balkans. An analysis of conceptual practices of power. *Anthropological Theory* 4, 1: 5-28.

Das, V., Kleinman, A.; Ramphele, M. & Reynolds, P.

2001 *Remaking a world. Violence, social suffering and recovering*. Berkeley: University of California Press.

Davis, John

1992 The anthropology of suffering. *Journal of Refugee Studies* 5, 2: 149-161.

De Swaan, A.

1982 *De mens is de mens een zorg*. Amsterdam: Meulenhoff.

Duras, M.

1985 *La Douleur*. Paris: P.O.L.

Fabian, J.

1983 *Time and the Other: How anthropology makes its object.* New York: Columbia University Press.

Ferreira, M. & E. van Dongen (eds)

2004 *Untold stories. Giving voice to older persons' lives in new South African society. An anthology*. Cape Town: The Albertina and Walter Sisulu Institute of Ageing in Africa, University of Cape Town.

Frankenberg, R.

1995 Learning from AIDS: The future of anthropology. In: Ahmed, A. & C. Shore (eds.), *The future of anthropology. Its relevance to the contemporary world.* London: Athlone, pp. 110-134.

Hinton, A.

2002 *Annilihating difference. The anthropology of genocide.* Berkeley: University of California Press.

Holmes Rhodes, E. & L. Holmes

1995 *Other cultures, elder years*. London: Sage.

Kleinman, A.

1995 *Writing at the margin. Discourse between anthropology and medicine.* Berkeley: University of California Press.

1998 Experience and its moral modes: Culture, human conditions, and disorder. Tanner Lectures. In: G. Peterson (ed.), *The Tanner lectures on human values*, Vol. 20. Salt Lake City: University of Utah Press, pp. 357-420.

Kovats-Bernat, J.

2002 Negotiating dangerous fields: Pragmatic strategies for fieldwork amid violence and terror. *American Anthropologist* 104, 1: 208-22.

Last, M.

2000 Reconciliation and memory in postwar Nigeria. In: A. Kleinman, V. Das, M. Raphele & P. Reynolds (eds.) *Violence and subjectivity*. Berkeley: University of California Press, pp. 315-333.

Malinowski, B.

1989 [1917] *A diary in the strict sense of the term*. London: Athlone Press.

Merleau-Ponty, M.

1973 The prose of the world. Evanston, Illinois: Northwestern University Press, pp. 133-134.

Moody-Adams, M.

1997 *Fieldwork in familiar places. Morality, culture & philosophy*. Cambridge/Mass: Harvard University Press.

Moore, H.

1995 *The future of anthropological knowledge*. London/New York: Routledge.

Nordstrom, C. & Robben, A. (eds)

1995 *Fieldwork under fire. Contemporary studies of violence and survival.* Berkeley: University of California Press.

Reynolds Whyte, S.

2003 *Anthropology of consequence: Problem and practice in a complex world.* Copenhagen: University of Copenhagen, inaugural lecture.

2005 Uncertain undertakings: Practicing health care in the subjunctive mood. In: V. Steffen, R. Jenkins & H. Jessen (eds.) *Managing uncertainty. Ethnographic studies of illness, risk and the struggle for control.* Copenhagen: Museum Tusculanum Press, pp. 245-265.

Robben, A.

1995 Seduction and persuasion. The politics of truth and emotion among victims and perpetrators of violence. In: Nordstrom, C. & A. Robben (eds) *Fieldwork under fire. Contemporary studies of violence and survival.* Berkeley: University of California Press, pp. 81-105.

Scheper-Hughes, N.

1995. The primacy of the ethical: Propositions for a militant anthropology. *Current Anthropology* 36, 3: 409-420.

Scheper-Hughes, N. & P. Bourgois, P.

2004 Introduction: Making sense of violence. In: N. Scheper-Hughes & P. Bourgois (eds.) *Violence in war and peace. An anthology.* Oxford: Blackwell Publishing, pp. 1-33.

Soyinka, W.

1999 *The burden of memory, the muse of forgiveness.* Oxford: Oxford University Press.

Spivak, G.

1988 Can the subaltern speak? Marxism and the interpretation of culture. In: C. Nelson & L. Grossberg (eds.) *Marxism and the interpretation of culture*. Urbana: University of Illinois Press, pp. 271-313.

Sturm, D.

1998 *Solidarity and suffering. Towards a politics of relationality*. New York: State University of New York Press.

Taussig, M.

1987 *Shamanism, colonialism and the white man: A study in terror and healing*. Chicago: University of Chicago Press.

Tobin, J.

1986 (Counter)transference and failure in intercultural therapy. *Ethos* 14, 2: 120-144.

Van Dongen, E.

2005a Musa ukuba yibokhwe ezigusheni: Social gerontocide in South Africa? *Medische Antropologie* 17, 1: 7-22.

2005b Remembering in times of misery: can older people in South Africa 'get through'? *Ageing and Society* 25, 4: 525-541.

Wenger, M.

1994 Idealism redux: The class-historical truth of postmodernism. *Critical Sociology* 20,1: 53-78.

Wolfe, A.

1989 *Whose keeper? Social science and moral obligation*. Berkeley: University of California Press.

## Witchcraft and violence: Aspects of distance and proximity

Ruth Kutalek & Armin Prinz

### Introduction

Witchcraft and magic or the occult have often been misunderstood by western science as something supernatural, metaphysical, bizarre and exotic. These phenomena, however, are a fundamental reality and existential truth for many people – they influence their modern daily lives. For them who experience witchcraft – either as victims or as accused – the encounter is very near and very real. Witchcraft is not a belief but a deep acknowledgement of facts which is embedded in society to an extent that sometimes makes us feel overwhelmed[6]. It is important to realize that people consider these phenomena an objective reality and that they have a strong impact on their lives. These phenomena are related to economic and political issues, to issues of gender and age and influence the health seeking behaviour of people, shortly, they influence the everyday decisions of people. They obviously used to have and in some circumstances still have, a sociologic, cultural and psychological function in society.

Living in Africa it is almost impossible not to be confronted with witchcraft. People talk about it. They relate that they lost their jobs because somebody interfered with witchcraft. They narrate that an old person was killed in his house last week because he was suspected to be a witch. They say that a person did not go to one's funeral and that this behaviour aroused suspicion. One can also read about witchcraft in newspapers. Almost every day there are columns or articles relating to it. One can buy witchcraft-horror-videos in the streets and watch them at home. People talk about witchcraft, sometimes behind raised hands, often laughing about it. A laughter that could mean as much as unbelievable, almost unwilling acceptance of the obvious reality. The phenomenon of witchcraft is experienced through all societal strata. Witchcraft discourses take place in everyday contexts (Ciekawy & Geschiere 1998), therefore these phenomena are so important when dealing with health and illness in Africa.

---

6 In 1971 a Cameroonian friend related to Geschiere: "I know that you Whites do not take sorcery seriously. That is why the colonial authorities left the witches alone. But now the state is run be Cameroonians. We Africans know that sorcery is all too real. Soon the lwa will be changed so that we can deal with these witches." (Geschiere and Fisiy 1994: 325)

In relation to the larger theme of this conference "Distance and proximity in times of illness" we want to show our own very personal apprehension relating to the topic "witchcraft and violence". While doing fieldwork in Congo (then Zaire) and Tanzania we were frequently confronted with witchcraft. We saw the victim's or accuser's side – patients and healers attributing illness or ill fate to occult powers – but often enough we also observed friends, informants or their relatives being accused to be witches. We saw the accusers and the accused and we saw the suffering involved on both sides.

In a way this contribution reflects our own helplessness when being confronted with witchcraft and violence. Undoubtedly these phenomena have to be seen in a context of economic and social uncertainties. People in Africa often have to live in conditions that a Western mind cannot even conceive: wars, violence, corruption, lack of infrastructure, food-crisis and often non-existent health providing systems.

We at times have the impression that anthropological research has distanced itself from many uncomfortable questions in this regard. How do we, as researcher, relate to the issue of witchcraft and violence? How do we react if we are told somebody has been killed because he was accused to be a witch? Is this a form of violence that should be seen in the context of "normal" domestic violence? How should we deal with these massive assaults towards women and, to a rising extent, towards children? What might be the causes for the increase of such phenomena in the last years?

Clearly, a lot of research has been done on witchcraft but little on how it actually affects people's lives and on how much they suffer. In this presentation we want to bring examples from Congo and Tanzania which bring the ones who are concerned into focus – patients and clients, accusers and accused. We bring narratives and stories that shook us and stirred many questions.

## Kaza basolo

*August 28, 1983, in Dungu, Northeast-Congo (former Zaire), in the tribal area of the Azande:*

Nako, a young Azande woman visits a small dispensary. She is very weak and has to be supported by her mother. With a flood of words the latter explains the complaints of her daughter to the European doctor. For a couple of weeks she has been suffering from a *kaza basolo*, an illness, which is caused by a bad person who has stolen her clitoris (*kaza* is illness, *basolo* means to scrape something away). Now she is in danger to loose her life. Her whole belly is hurting and she is in risk to bleed to death. She is not able to walk alone any more and in an upright position she is nearly fainting. The doctor examines the patient. The belly is soft, only a small, abscess-like formation is to be seen at hand's breadth left to the navel. The genital area, besides a menstruation-like bleeding, is without noticeable alteration. The doctor tries to explain them that there are no pathological findings, especially the clitoris is absolutely normal, but all in vain. Undiscerning to his opinion, both of them persist on the story of the stolen clitoris. To calm them down he orders to do the in bushclinics usual laboratory examinations: blood-smear, blood-count, haemoglobin, faeces and urine for parasites. The results were negative besides a considerable anaemia, which cannot be explained by the discovered low and for this area common infection with hookworms in the stool (Prinz 1998).

The illness episode relates to a secret Azande society[7] of hunters and fisherman called *aboro basolo*. To achieve better hunting success members of this society conduct magic practices for which, according to Azande conception, they need a clitoris. They "steal" the clitoris by shaking hands with an unsuspecting woman. Her clitoris then "moves" over the arms into a small leather bag containing magical plants, which is worn by the wrongdoer on his belt. Back at home he is said to carbonize its contents – the plants and the imagery clitoris –, he then mixes the ashes with magical oils and smears the substance on his hunting weapons. The woman who believes to be robbed of her clitoris reacts with panic. Her menstruation will be disturbed, she will complain of pain in the belly, the articulations and muscles, she might suffer from certain forms of dermatitis. Restlessness, panic-attacks and social disorders are sure to appear.

In rare cases also men are said to become victim of *basolo*. They believe that their penis has been stolen and start to have similar health problems as the sick women. Although the penis is in fact still present, for the victim it has vanished. A penis, however, is not very desired for the magic preparation

---

[7] Secret societies are very common among the Azande, its members are known to be very powerful. They are founded for political reasons but also for the economic benefit of their members. Their members are practising special magical rituals in order to enhance the feeling of social unity. These societies are often subject to a frequent change and of only local importance. Sometimes only a few decades later nothing is known about the existence of a society that was described as important by early anthropologists. Evans-Pritchard (1931), for instance, reported about the *mani* society which, at his time, was immensely important politically as a resistance movement against chiefs who collaborated with the colonial authorities. Nowadays, however, hardly anybody can remember it anymore.

because the sorcerer is bound to catch only "strong" animals like leopards and lions which are without any economical value for the hunter. *Kaza basolo* can also be transmitted by the consumption of meat from animals which were hunted by means of this magic. In this case no "genital bleeding" occurs but severe belly pain, vomiting and bloody diarrhea.

For the Azande *kaza basolo*[8] is a reality in day-to-day life. It is described in such a genuine way that Christian missionaries still believe that the Azande are actually practising clitoridectomy.

### *Treatment and prophylaxis of kaza basolo*

If a woman feels that she has been attacked by a *boro basolo* she will first try to get back the stolen genital from the sorcerer before he is able to carbonize it. Hereto she asks the help of her relatives to find the suspected person by means of oracles. The oracles among the Azande have a hierarchic order which depend on the kind of oracle and the social status of the diviner (Evans-Pritchard 1937: 352 ff.). The highest-ranking oracle is the famous poison oracle *benge*, which is also used as an ordeal at the tribal court. If the minor oracles, which are conducted by old family members of the victim, have detected a suspicious person who refuses to confess his guilt, she will go to the diviner of the tribal court to confirm the first finding through the poison oracle. If this is also positive the detected sorcerer has to accept his guilt and is forced by the society to give back the stolen organ. Additionally he is punished with prison.

Not always is the solution of the problem solved that easily. In most cases time is not sufficient to detect the evildoer before he has burned the genital. Now only very special healers, the *abinza basolo*, are able to treat the symptoms of the illness. But since the genital has been already "destroyed", no treatment is able to cure the victim completely. Because of this defect she is always in danger to die suddenly. This involves a permanent handicap that deprives the woman of a normal day-to-day life.

---

[8] According to the ethnopsychiatric taxonomy of Culture-Bound-Syndromes *basolo* can be subsumed to the so-called Genital Retraction Taxons (Simons & Hughes 1985). The basic of this taxon is the fear of loosing ones sexuality, a fear that is universal to humans but is manifested in different forms. The main syndrome of this taxon is the Penis Retraction Syndrome *koro* from East-Asia and Africa (Edwards 1984, Ilechukwu 1992, Jilek 1986, Mather 2005). According to Yap (1977) *koro* is a "culture-conditioned acute depersonalization syndrome".

As this syndrome in some areas of Zande-Land, especially around the town of Dungu, is very frequent and involves the greater part of society, a general frenzied reaction is only logical. As a problematic kind of avoidance of this syndrome some people already restrain from shaking hands – thus evoking social isolation, for this habit is an important part of Zande communication. When meeting someone in the street, when entering into a house where several people are present, as a sign of courtesy one has to greet by shaking hands with everybody. Now that people where so much afraid of this disease, nobody dared to shake hands anymore, an atmosphere of distrust arouse, the social harmony was disrupted.

Even if Zande people show a clear respect towards witchcraft and sorcery it is not that they are helplessly exposed to their fears and horrors. A specific prophylaxis is executed by some healers, who in large-scale programs similar to Western type campaigns, traditionally "vaccinate" the population. Special wild onions are carbonized, powdered and mixed with peanut-oil. This paste is rubbed into scarification scars made with a razor blade between thumb and forefinger. Then the healer wraps an armband made of savanna grass around the wrist, takes in deep concentration both hands of the patient into his and appeals to his ancestors to defend his protégé against the *aboro basolo*. Apart from interpretations that *kaza basolo* is a manifestation of gender problems, the patients who are suffering experience this condition as an enormous disturbance of their health conditions. For them it is a reality, influencing their social, economic and cultural life.

We are often asked if people really believe that *kaza basolo* can cause death? And we have to answer that there are myriads of possibilities to die in Africa. Treatable infectious diseases such as malaria, acute respiratory infections and Aids are responsible for many deaths in Sub-Saharan Africa. Through the disastrous economic and political situation in Congo (but also in many other African countries) and a complete breakdown in infrastructure there is virtually no working health care system in the country. Especially in rural areas there are no doctors and no nurses and often the most basic medicines are missing. The few antimalarials, painkillers and antibiotics which are available are mostly smuggled from Uganda. They are more often than not of questionable quality and in any case unaffordable to the majority. If people become severely sick they often die. As we understand it, witchcraft is a way to have control over a situation that is otherwise too unbearable. From the people's perspective it is quite clear: against witchcraft something can be done, against disease they are helpless.

## Witchcraft and society

*November 13, 1997, in Kibena, Southwest Tanzania. The mother of a young pregnant woman consults the traditional healer Lutumo.*

healer: Where is your husband?

mother: He is at home.

healer (consults his divination bottle): The pregnancy started long ago.

mother: We sent her to hospital.

healer: It is not malaria or so, she is pregnant, she suffered quite often, sometimes feeling better.

mother: Yes.

healer: (consults his rubbing oracle) She started suffering from here (point to his belly). Where is her husband?

mother: He is at home, he is very young.

healer: The woman needs to get the baby out. She suffers but she can't give birth. (He consults his rubbing board again) The baby has been tied up inside the womb.

mother: Please help me!

healer: The baby can't turn to the other side because it she has been tied up. If this woman goes to the hospital, the only solution will be the knife.

mother: Please help me!

healer: Where do you come from?

mother: We come from Ibiki.

healer: The child has been tied up. The one who did that is not a man, she is a woman.

mother: Is she a young or an old woman?

healer: An old woman. (He consults his rubbing board) The one who witched her is a woman. Therefore your daughter needs to be operated. If they make an operation your daughter and the child will die.

(to his assistant Salingwa) Do we have makasi (a plant)?

healer's assistant: It is there.

mother: Please tell me who that woman is.

healer: Where is the husband of your daughter? Is the husband of her present, did he come?

mother: He is at home, but my daughter is outside here.

healer: That old woman was feeling jealous because that young man has married her granddaughter. Your family-side is the very one which bewitched your daughter. That's why they tied up the child. Look at that one (he points to the moving oracle), it has moved to your side, do you see it?

mother: Yes.

healer: (consults his rubbing board) Why doesn't that old woman want that the child should be married?

mother: I don't know, but she liked her to stay at home without being married.

healer: Why that old woman disliked her grandchild to be married? It is unusual to hear about this. Your old grandmother is a hopeless woman. She is a witch.

mother: Please help me!

healer: (the rubbing oracle moves under the table) Look, this thing is moving the way you came from. It goes where the witch is (He takes a stick and collects the oracle). The grandmother didn't like her grandchild to be married by that young man. She didn't like the side of the husband.

mother: According to what she said it is true. She is unhappy that her granddaughter is married to that man.

healer (to his assistant): Take lyan'gambi and makasi and mlali (different kinds of medicine). Ponder makasi and boil the other medicine and give it to her.

(He consults his rubbing board again)

research assistant (Mr. Kyando): Why did the grandmother tie her up?

healer: She didn't like the man to marry her, so she would be staying with her.

mother: She doesn't like her to be married.

research assistant: Does your daughter stay with her grandmother or with you?

mother: My daughter stays with me, not with her grandmother. My mother is feeling shy, she asks herself: „Why is my granddaughter married by a head teacher?“ That's why she is feeling unhappy.

healer: (consults his rubbing board): That old woman is a witch. It is the one who tied up the child in the stomach. If you knew that your daughter had been in trouble for such a long time, you would have come here to me before going to the hospital.

mother: My daughter is just outside, let me check where she is.

healer: Call her, she should come inside.

The above case study is only an example of how interpretations of witchcraft can be formed during a healing setting. In often endless narratives would a patient explain to the traditional healer Lutumo what his problems were and he in return would give advice on how the matter could be tackled in the best way. In most of the cases, the patient's stories circulate around the issues of illness, relationships and economic problems. What is so intriguing is that almost all the episodes brought before Lutumo in one way or another are dealing with issues of witchcraft (Kutalek 2001).

Witchcraft accusations often take place within the family; that is why healers always try to bring together family members, even if, as in this case, they live far away from each other. Ciekawy & Geschiere (1998: 4) state that "in many parts of Africa witchcraft is linked to 'home' and to the 'family'" and that "witchcraft can be characterized as the dark side of kinship". A witch usually does not attack people from outside her or his lineage or village (see Colson 2000); "witchcraft is an intimate act" (Bastian 1993: 134). In van der Geest's (2002) article on old age in Ghana one of his Akan informants relates: "The elders say 'It is your clansman who kills you. It is someone from your house who kills you.'" Another protagonist reports on a proverb which is commonly applied to witchcraft, "If an insect bites you, it is from your own cloth." (ibid.: 446 f.)

Witchcraft has something to do with social distance and proximity because the closer a person is socially the easier is the bewitchment. It also has something to do with physical proximity – the nearer a witch lives physically with his or her victim the easier it is for him or her to harm. Among the Azande classical witchcraft, in contrary to magic, is only effective while being physically close, whereas magic practices, for which *kaza basolo* is an example, can also be effective if somebody is in distance physically and socially. This is the reason why Zande traditionally prefer to settle in homesteads that lie far away from each other. To escape witchcraft attacks people also repeatedly leave their home villages to resettle in other areas.

In the triangle Sudan, Congo (former Zaire) and Central African Republic the head of the collectivité Wando, Constant Lungagbe Mbatanadu, is a former Catholic brother. People frequently complained about witches, but as he was a former brother he was not supposed to believe in such things. Nonetheless, for his people (and presumably "inofficially" also for him) witchcraft was experienced as a major problem and he had to find a solution. In former times witches would have been punished for their evil deeds but as a former priest of a church, which did not accept their existence in the first place, he obviously could not do so. What he did was the following: he had a village built far away from his people's compounds and had all people, who were convicted witches (by the local court) and their families brought there. From now on they had to live there and as the witches' village was far away they would not be able to harm his people anymore. As a punishment they had to work for the general public. Because witchcraft is only active during night, they had to walk home to their "exile" in the evening. Whenever somebody from that village dies, people from the area are relieved and even celebrate his death[9].

At least in former times it seems that witchcraft discourses had the ability to act out social inequalities and tensions, especially in times of uncertainties and crisis. "Wheras older, rural discourses and practices related to witchcraft thus ultimately strengthened kinship solidarity and acted as local forms of conflict prevention and resolution, the newly emerging discursive formations surrounding witchcraft in the urban context contribute, on the contrary, to the weakening of kinship ties in rather dramatic ways." (De Boeck & Plissart 2004: 197)

Witchcraft seems to change its pattern rapidly. It takes on the one hand a more impersonal quality which does not necessarily afflict close kin – as we have seen in the case of *kaza basolo*. On the other hand it seems to move to models that were previously not known at all, as shows the example of the massive appearance of child witches in Kinshasa (see below).

---

[9] Similar witch sanctuaries, where accused witches are banished to live, are also known from Ghana (Adinkrah 2004).

## Witchcraft, violence, poverty and control

*Outrageous witchcraft murders in Makete (The Guardian, Tanzania)*

"Seven people have been brutally murdered and seven others severely wounded with pangas (a kind of matchet), spears and other crude weapons in a series of attacks linked to witchcraft in Makete District, Iringa Region. Revealing this, Iringa Regional Police Commander Omar Mganga said the incidents took place in Ndao, Nungu and Kinyika villages in Makete District, towards the end of last month. According to police investigations, a few days before the killings, some villagers conducted a secret ballot to unearth suspects thought to be involved in witchcraft. The RPC said on July 20 at night, more than ten youths armed with spears, sharp pieces of metal, pangas, and other crude weapons like bows and arrows, invaded Ndapo Village, killing one person and wounding another. On July 25, the marauding youths attacked Nungu Village at around 10.00pm and killed three people and wounded four others. Three people were killed and two others wounded in a similar attack conducted between July 27 and 28 at Kinyika Village, he added. Later on, a group of villagers gave marching orders to all people involved in witchcraft in the villages. According to the RPC, some suspected witches vacated the villages fearing for their lives. He mentioned the deceased as (six names of mostly elderly men are revealed, one woman was in her forties) Twenty-two people have been arrested in connection with what he described as "tragic killings" in the wake of a manhunt mounted by the Police Force in the region. The arrested suspects were found with a list of names of more people the villagers suspected to be witches and wizards [22 suspects are listed with their full names, 2 of them are female] They are all in police custody and soon they will be charged for murder. Police are continuing with the crackdown to nab all the suspects involved to control the situation." (Mvungi 2004)

On April 8, 2001 the Sunday Observer reported that on the previous day 31 people were killed along the Mbeya-Tunduma road (Southwest Tanzania) after an overloaded minibus crashed into another stationary bus at high speed. One villager said that "The driver of the mini-bus lost control, veered off the road and somersaulted before hitting the stationary bus." The next day the following article under the headline *Manhunt still on: Mbeya people lynch men connected with road crash* appeared:

"A resident of Songwe where a commuter mini-bus plying the Mbeya-Tunduma route rammed into a stationary bus and killed 33 people, has been lynched by an angry mob claiming he was behind the ghastly accident. The

Mbeya Regional Police Commander, Laurean Sanya, said yesterday the old man, who has not been identified yct, was killed yesterday by people who believed he caused the accident by witchcraft. Earlier, one Sola Jongolo was also lynched in connection with the accident. He was killed shortly after he was seen collecting brains of people killed in the accident and putting them in a plastic bag. It was claimed he was working jointly with three residents in the area who are also being hunted. Sanya said the police had received reports of the killings of the people said to have caused the accident by witchcraft. It is said Songwe residents do not believe the accident was caused by a speeding vehicle whose driver lost control and rammed into a parked bus. The mob was hunting for other old men believed to have worked together with Jongolo and the unidentified lynched old man said to have caused the accident. Thirty-three people, including a driver of a commuter mini-bus plying the Mbeya-Tunduma route died after it rammed into a Tawfiq stationary bus on Saturday morning in Songwe area." (PST Correspondent 2001)

Rumours and stories about witchcraft express deep anxiety. It is obvious that witchcraft needs some kind of socially accepted control. There exists an urgent need for people to find forms of containment, the need to look for ways to "neutralize" or "domesticate" these dangerous forces (Ciekawy & Geschiere 1998). In some societies anti-witchcraft movements experience a revitalisation (Auslander 1993, Röschenthaler 2004) in others the state is demanded to intervene (Geschiere & Fisiy 1994). Witchcraft, however, is violence experienced in two ways. By people who were from their standpoint unfairly accused, on the one hand, it is violence experienced as any domestic or community violence is felt. It is on the other hand felt as an evil intrusion by the people who think they were bewitched, as was shown in the two case studies from Congo and Tanzania. For the afflicted victims, unjustly accusations are a category that virtually do not exist. Somebody has made them ill so that they now stand on the verge to death; for them it is a traumatic experience to fall sick due to witchcraft. "The sufferers are cast to the realm of death" as Bruce Kapferer (2004) fittingly put it. Fear of witchcraft prompts the people to leave their houses, villages and jobs.

Witchcraft in its wider discussion on violence and public health is clearly underrepresented in scientific research. People accused of being sorcerers or witches fall victim to its often severe consequences ranging from severe humiliation to homicide. Witchcraft is an extremely complex matter because it is related to sensitive social and cultural issues such as age, gender, status, economic uncertainties and religion. Violence in relation to witchcraft is an issue that is hardly publicly discussed, taboo and secret because it leaves us too uneasy and helpless to deal with it professionally. Violence upsets us. It makes us feel helpless and at loss. Because everybody has experienced violence in one or the other form in his own life, discussions on violence are often led very emotionally.

In 1996 the World Health Assembly has declared violence to be a leading worldwide public health problem (WHO 2002). The World Health Organization defines violence as: "The intentional use of physical force or power, threatened or actual, against oneself, another person, or against a group or community, that either results in or has a high likelihood of resulting in injury, death, psychological harm, maldevelopment or deprivation." (WHO 2002: 4) Violent behaviour threatens the lives, health and well-being of individuals and communities. Because the costs of violence to a high proportion result from its impact on the victim's health, understanding its causes and setting prevention measures are key issues for public health institutions. Violence is a particularly sensitive problem because it 1) touches on issues of culture and morality 2) it relates to matters of age, gender and economic status and 3) it provokes uncomfortable emotions which range from helplessness to anger.

In 2000 approximately 520.000 people were killed in acts of interpersonal violence worldwide (WHO 2002: 13). There are not even estimations on how many people were killed, injured or otherwise harmed in relation to witchcraft accusations. In northern Nigeria a study among offenders in a Nigerian federal prison showed that 13,3 % of victims that were killed in circumstances of one-to-one activity were in relation to witchcraft allegations (Mafullul 2000). Data on homicide related to witchcraft are difficult to get because as there is frequently close kin involved, cases are mostly not reported to the police (Adinkrah 2004, Ogembo 2001). As accusations of witchcraft frequently have to be suffered by the elderly, the poor or by women and children, victims often do not report violent acts. "... the poor are not only more likely to suffer, they are also more likely to have their suffering silenced." (Farmer 1997: 280). It seems that an increase of social and economic uncertainties leads to a rise in number and severity of accusations.

In former times the control of witchcraft laid in the hands of the individual and the community. If somebody thought he became victim of witchcraft he could consult a traditional practitioner who took care of protective or counteractive medicine. At a community level the witch could be forced to reveal his or her identity. In Southwest Tanzania and in Northeast Congo – as in many other parts of Africa – this could be achieved by a poison ordeal[10]. Among the Bena the nominal punishment for the practice of witchcraft was death. In practice, however, it was difficult to prove the charge before the *mtema* (chief of the area). In cases that were hard to decide he would order the poison ordeal which both the accuser and the accused had to drink[11]. This practice naturally limited accusations by itself. The Bena therefore usually refrained to "private methods" of warding off supernatural attacks by using counter-magic (Culwick & Culwick 1935). As poison ordeals were forbidden by colonial administrations this form of protection in most cases is done until today.

Since the 1930s anti-sorcery and anti-witchcraft movements are appearing irregularly in East, South and Central-Africa. These movements "have emerged to fill the gap in society's defences against mystical enemies left by the suppression of the poison ordeal by colonial governments" (Willis 1968: 11). In the 1960s, for instance, members of the well-known Kamcape movement in Ufipa in Southwest Tanzania would undertake "cleansing" operations in several villages. The accused witches were publicly humiliated and "branded" with large double crosses incised on their foreheads (Willis 1968: 9).

Auslander (1993) reports of a relatively recent movement in the 1980s in Eastern Zambia. The witchfinder, who would call himself "doctor" would line up the inhabitants of a village in two rows. In one line stood the males, beginning with the youngest and ending with the oldest, in the other line stood the females in the very same way. One at a time they were called to stand in a circle which was drawn in the sand to be "examined" by the witchfinder. Each received a digit which stood for the number of marks that should be incised onto his or her upper chest by a disciple of the witchfinder. Most of the young girls and boys received a low digit between one and ten. As the interrogation moved to the old people, especially the women, it became more ferocious. The huts of the suspected were searched for incriminating objects like magic horns which are thought to be able to afflict and kill people. They became subject to violent treatment with incisions all over their bodies, beating and humiliations. The age and the gender aspect are particularly obvious in these performances. One village described by

---

10 Among the Azande the poison ordeal *benge* was done with humans in former times, later they were substituted with young chicken (Prinz 1978)

11 In some cases either or both substituted a slave to take the poison for him (Culwick & Culwick 1935: 212)

Auslander (ibid. 172) is renowned for its especially independent women who earn their living as entrepreneurs and smugglers. The invitation of the witch-finder to a village, which was often supported by young male villagers, always provoked bitter and prolonged controversy. Except in one case, however, there was no noteworthy resistance. The old people were often held responsible for miscarriages, sickness – especially Aids –, death and the failure by young men to prosper. The gerontocratic authority was challenged. Anti-witchcraft movements are thus taking a clear political and social dimension. The victims are often left deeply traumatized by the violent ceremonies and public humiliation, even if Auslander states that "most appeared to recuperate with time" (ibid.186).

In the Southwest of Cameroon the famous witchfinder Aching in 1999 related that torture is indispensable in witchcraft accusations, without it the people would not reveal anything. His only aim was that the people would stop doing evil things to each other. Only after they were tortured for four hours would they start to confess. After each confession he would pray and preach for them and after four weeks they would refrain from thinking bad things (Röschenthaler 2004: 132).

Frequently it is elderly women accused of witchcraft (Ferreira 2004, Forrester-Kibuga 1999), as is the case in our Tanzanian example where the grandmother of the young woman was detected a witch. These accusations can lead to severe violence towards women, as many authors have illustrated (e.g. Adinkrah 2004, Auslander 1993, Bastian 1993, Mesaki 1994, Ogembo 2001). In addition to being physically abused and socially rejected, these women often suffer material and financial neglect from their close relatives. Adinkrah (2004) reports of 14 cases of homicide in the years 1995-2001 in Ghana, reviewed in the daily issue of a newspaper. These cases are only the tip of the iceberg because homicide within close kin is often not reported, and some witch killings might have been misclassified as accidents or suicides. Of the 14 instances of homicidal aggression 13 were women; most offenders were males[12]. Typically persecutions take place in times of crisis

---

[12] It is also interesting to note that out of 10 cases described by Adinkrah four cases involved a previous consultation of a charismatic or healing church member. Charismatic Christian movements seem to be not seldomly involved in violence related to witchcraft. A few weeks before a witchcraft associated lynching took place in Keera region, Kenya, several Christian preachers organized "evangelistic crusades", calling upon witches to "give up their witchcraft lest a fire consume them" (Ogembo 2001: 10) Christian fundamentalist churches, predominantly the Pentecoastal churches, are currently mushrooming in many parts of Africa. Since their arrival in Africa in the early 20th century, the preacher's activities were always connected to witchcraft-cleansing activities (van Dijk 2001: 100), often building on "traditional" anti-witchcraft movements.

or misfortune. In 1997 three middle-aged women were killed by an angry mob who accused the women of being involved in a meningitis epidemic (ibid.: 343).

## Child witches and violence towards young people

A press clipping from Uganda reports the following:

*Children held over ritual murder*

"Police in Kapchorwa on Tuesday arrested five suspects over the murder of a boy whose mutilated body was found in a river. The district police commander, Tomson Ogole, said the suspects were arrested in London Bridge village, in Kapchorwa town council. They were swimming at the spot where the corpse was recovered on Monday, he added. Ogole said an 11-year-old suspect is on the run. The deceased was a pupil of Kapchorwa Modern Boarding Primary School. Ogole said the deceased is believed to have been strangled by the assailants. The also cut off his lips, ear and private parts in what is suspected to have been a ritual sacrifice." (…) (Muzungyo 2003)

Contrary to some of the more "traditional" forms of witchcraft manifestations, accusations towards young people and even small children are a phenomenon that in some parts of Africa have taken a considerable extent[13]. In former times witchcraft was often associated with old age. The older a witch the more powerful he or she usually was considered. Especially among the Azande it was believed that through age the organ of witchcraft, which is thought to lie in the lower belly, grows and thus becomes more powerful. Interpretations of witchcraft in modernity, however, seem to undergo a massive change.

Filip de Boeck (2004) reports of a video which he got by chance in 1994. In the film three Zairian children, aged between 8 and 12 who lived in Brussels, the Zairian Diaspora, were interrogated by several adults and two Belgiums, members of a Pentecoste praying movement. The children recently arrived in Belgium from Zaire. The film shows how they were accused of the death of several relatives. In the course of the interrogation which was at times quite violent, the children admitted to have "eaten" several people in Kinshasa.

---

[13] Contrary to this is the typical and indeed widespread accusation that witches kill young children or cause abortions, thus threatening the reproduction of an ethnic group (see as examples van der Geest 2002: 449 for Ghana, Burke 2000 for Botswana and Pradelles de Latour 1995 for Cameroon)

They reported how they left their bodies to fly to Kinshasa where they were helped by elder witches and friends. In the end they give a macabre description how they killed their victims, chopped them up and distributed body parts to their friends. The video was later sent to the relatives of the children in Kinshasa to confirm aroused suspicions.

De Boeck confirms that in 1999 such stories were frequent in cities like Kinshasa. Until now many children are involved in comparable rumours and suspicions and many of them are forced on the streets; nowadays street children are a normal sight in all parts of the city. Such accusations towards children within their own families are widespread despite all ethnic and social boundaries. Repeatedly children between 4 and 18 years old are accused of causing accidents, mishappenings, or illness and death of other children or adults within the family or neighbourhood. Frequently these children provoke massive conflict within the family, often they are severely beaten or even killed (De Boeck 2004: 32 ff.).

De Boeck & Plissart argue that fundamentalist churches play an "ambivalent role", in that they are part of the witchcraft problem itself but also provide a local solution to this problem. However, the question has to be posed, if the churches which are undertaking these deliverings are not fostering these occult realities through their accepting them. They demonise witches, exorcise the accused and by that, signal to the outside that they accept these phenomena as real. De Boeck & Plissart (2004: 174) report that children are brought by their parents so that they publicly confess. Up to one hundred children are accepted for "treatment" every week. For weeks and even months they have to undergo a period of seclusion. In this time they are frequently interrogated and also abused by the priests. For fear of their witchcraft, these children later are often rejected by their parents. One has to ask if this can be called a "local solution".

Witchcraft beliefs do not become less relevant with increased education or modernization[14]. The ideas undergo changes in that manifestations of witchcraft seem to alter to less "traditional" ones.

---

[14] In contrast, Adinkrah is of the opinion that "higher rates of literacy and modernization in Ghana's urban areas appear to modulate witch beliefs to some degree (p. 349) and that "formal education may have the potential of eradicating such beliefs" (p. 350).

## Epilogue

If we approach the kaleidoscope of witchcraft, magic or the occult it is obvious that there is no clear-cut and easy way to understand these phenomena. This is underlined by the fact that the distinction between good and evil in the discussion of witchcraft is sometimes not so clear as we wish it to be (Geschiere & Fisiy 1994). Even if witchcraft per se is often perceived as something utterly evil, there also exist concepts of "good" or at least legitimated witchcraft (Janzen 1982: 49; van der Geest 2002: 455 ff.). A traditional healer in Tanzania might go so far as to say that through social misbehaviour evil forces can actually be invited in one's house, thus rendering the question of who is seen to be "guilty" or "victim" highly ambivalent. In some cases witchcraft might be a justifiable form of punishing somebody (Kutalek 2001: 112ff.). Moreover, healing and witchcraft are not necessarily contradictory qualities. The academic distinction between witchcraft and healing is often not reality in African day-to-day life. Traditional healers are often simultaneously denoted as witches, they are able to heal or to do harm. Indeed, to efficiently treat somebody afflicted by witchcraft it is necessary to possess the same powers as the evildoer. A good healer is respected for his powers that are initially seen as ambivalent. It is largely a matter of standpoint if they are considered as good or evil. In some societies witchcraft, even if perceived as something utterly evil, is at the same time seen to be "a precondition of success and authority" (Geschiere & Fisiy 1994: 334). Also the traditional authorities are part of this system. "The chief partakes of the same power as the witch, with the difference that the witch uses it for selfish ends and the destruction of the collectivity, or even to benefit a witchcraft coven, while the chief exercises mystical power and even capital punishment upon individual subjects for the collective good." (Janzen 1982: 24) Not only poor and vulnerable people are accused of practising witchcraft but also prosperous and socially well embedded. It also seems that witchcraft increasingly takes place on an economic level where status and money become more important (Comaroff & Comaroff 1999).

When dealing with witchcraft in Africa there is the clear danger of "exoticizing Africa" (Ciekawy & Geschiere 1998: 1), of telling spectacular stories without reflecting on economic, political or social uncertainties. Africa for a long time has been considered the continent of "superstition" and witchcraft. When people are suffering they often make occult forces responsible. We should realize that in the face of social change, economic hardship and virtually non-existing medical facilities for the majority this might be one way to have control over suffering.

**References**

Adinkrah, M.

2004 Witchcraft accusations and female homicide victimization in contemporary Ghana. *Violence Against Women* 10, 4: 325-356.

Auslander, M.

1993 "Open the wombs!" The symbolic politics of modern Ngoni witchfinding. In: J. Comaroff & J. Comaroff (eds.) *Modernity and its malcontents. Ritual and power in postcolonial Africa.* Chicago: The University of Chicago Press, pp. 167-192.

Bastian, Misty L.

1993 "Bloodhounds who have no friends": Witchcraft and locality in the Nigerian popular press. In: J. Comaroff & J. Comaroff (eds.) *Modernity and its malcontents. Ritual and power in postcolonial Africa.* Chicago: The University of Chicago Press, pp. 129-166.

Burke, Ch.

2000 They cut Segametsi into part: Ritual murder, youth, and the politics of knowledge in Botswana. *Anthropological Quarterly* 73, 4: 204-214.

Ciekawy, D. & Geschiere, P.

1998 Containing witchcraft: conflicting scenarios in postcolonial Africa. *African Studies Review* 41, 3: 1-14.

Colson, E.

2000 The father as witch. *Africa* 70, 3: 333-358.

Culwick, A.T. and Culwick, G.M.

1935 *Ubena of the rivers*. London: George Allen and Unwin.

De Boeck, Filip

2004 Die zweite Welt. Kinder und Hexerei in der Demokratischen Republik Kongo. In: T. Wendl (ed.) *Africa screams. Das Böse in Kino, Kunst und Kult*. Wuppertal: Peter Hammer Verlag, pp. 31-47.

De Boeck, F. & Plissart, M.-F.

2004 *Kinshasa. Tales of the invisible city*. Ghent, Amsterdam: Ludion.

Edwards J.W.

1984 Indigenous koro, a genital retraction syndrome of insular Southeast Asia: A critical review. *Culture, Medicine and Psychiatry* 8, 1-24.

Evans-Pritchard, E.E.

1931 Mani, a Zande secret society. *Sudan Notes and Records* 14: 105-148.

1937 Witchcraft, oracles and magic among the Azande. Oxford: Clarendon Press.

Farmer, P.

1997 On suffering and structural violence. A view from below. In: A. Kleinman, V. Das & M. Lock (eds.) Social suffering. Berkeley, Los Angeles, London: University of California Press, pp. 261-283

Ferreira, M.

2004 Elder abuse in Africa: What policy and legal provisions are there to address the violence? *Journal of Elder Abuse and Neglect* 16, 2: 17-32

Forrester Kibuga, K.

1999 Wisdom and witchery. *The Courier* 176, July, August, 66-67

Geschiere, P. & Fisiy, C.

1994 Domesticating personal violence: witchcraft, courts and confessions in Cameroon. *Africa* 64, 3: 323-341.

Ilechukwu, S.T.C.

1992 Magical penis loss in Nigeria: Report of a recent epidemic of a koro-like syndrome. *Transcultural Psychiatric Research Review* 29, 2: 91-108

Janzen, J.

1982 *The quest for therapy. Medical pluralism in lower Zaire.* Berkeley: University of California Press.

Jilek, W.G.

1986 Epidemis of "genital shrinking" (koro): Historical review and report of a recent outbreak in South China. *Curare* 9, 269-282.

Kapferer, B.

2004 *The phenomenology of embodiment and the practice of theory.* Lecture held at the 8th Biennial Easa Conference "Face to Face. Connecting distance and proximity", Vienna, September 8-12, 2004.

Kutalek, R.

2001 *Steven Lihonama Lutumo. Leben und Arbeit eines traditionellen Heilers der Bena Südwest Tansanias.* Berlin: Verlag für Wissenschaft und Bildung.

Mafullul, Y.M.

2000 Homicide in northern Nigeria: An evaluation of motives. *American Journal of Forensic Psychiatry* 21, 1: 69-76.

Mather, C.

2005 Accusations of genital theft: a case from northern Ghana. *Culture, Medicine and Psychiatry* 29: 33-52.

Mesaki, S.

1994 Witch-killing in Sukumaland. In: R. Abrahams (ed.) *Witchcraft in contemporary Tanzania.* Cambridge: African Studies Centre, University of Cambridge, pp. 47-60.

Muzungyo, R.

2003 Children held over ritual murder. *The New Vision*, February 21, p. 8

Mvungi, A.

2004 Outragous witchcraft murders in Makete. *The Guardian* (Tanzania), August 3, p. 1

Ogembo, J. M.

2001 Cultural narratives, violence, and mother-son loyality: an exploration into Gusii personification of evil. *Ethos* 29, 1: 3-29.

Pradelles de Latour, C.-H.

1995 Witchcraft and the avoidance of physical violence in Cameroon. *Journal of the Royal Anthropological Institute* (N.S.) 1: 599-609.

Prinz, A.

1978 Gift-Orakel. Film E 2380 des IWF. *Publ.Wiss.Film., Sekt. Ethnol.*, Ser.8, Nr.19, 18 S. Göttingen (Germany).

1998 "*Kaza basolo*" – A culture-bound syndrome among the Azande of Northeast-Congo. In: Ch. E. Gottschalk-Batschkus & Ch. Rätsch (eds.) *Ethnotherapien: Therapeutische Konzepte im Kulturvergleich. Curare Sonderband* 14, Berlin: VWB, pp. 53-57.

PST Correspondent

2001 Manhunt still on: Mbeya people lynch men connected with road crash. *The Guardian* (Tanzania), April 9, p. 1.

Röschenthaler, U.

2004 Die Ambivalenz des Außerordentlichen. Talent und Macht als endliche Ressource in Cross-River-Gebiet. In: T. Wendl (ed.) *Africa screams. Das Böse in Kino, Kunst und Kult.* Wuppertal: Peter Hammer Verlag, pp. 127-141

Simons, R. & Hughes, C.

1985 *The culture-bound syndromes. Folk illnesses of psychiatric and anthropological interest.* Dordrecht, Boston, Lancaster, Tokyo: D. Reidel Publishing Company.

Van der Geest, S.

2002 From wisdom to witchcraft: ambivalence towards old age in rural Ghana. *Africa* 72, 3: 437-463.

Van Dijk, R.

2001 Witchcraft and scepticism by proxy. Pentecoastalism and laughter in urban Malawi. In: H. Moore & T. Sanders (eds.) *Magical interpretations, material realities. Modernity, witchcraft and the occult in postcolonial Africa.* London: Routledge, pp. 97-117.

Willis, R.G.

1968 Kamcape: an anti-sorcery movement in south-west Tanzania. *Africa* 38, 1: 1-15.

WHO

2002 *World report on violence and health.* Geneva: World Health Organization

Yap, P.M.

[1969] 1977 The culture-bound reactive syndromes. In: D. Landy (ed.) *Culture, disease and healing.* New York: Macmillan, pp. 340-349.

# Face to face with refugee women's distress in the Netherlands: Distance and proximity in the aftermath of sexual violence

Annemiek Richters, Marian Tankink, Hishamah Bel Khodja, Janus Oomen and Marianne Cense

## Introduction

Sexual violence perpetrated in the context of violent conflicts and their aftermath is increasingly being recognized internationally as a serious traumatic event that may have major impacts on the health and well-being of the women affected by it. Accordingly, human rights activists and humanitarian agencies working in conflict and post-conflict regions have begun to pay specific attention to survivors of sexual violence in these areas. In asylum procedures, the experience of sexual violence is also singled out for consideration. If refugee women can prove that they have been exposed to sexual violence in the countries from which they have escaped, there is a chance that they may be granted asylum in the country in which they seek safety. These various processes of recognition have been accompanied by a growing body of research focusing on the function and meaning of sexual violence in the context of war, the way women experience the violence, its impact on women's physical and psychological health, and the health care and psychosocial and legal assistance necessary to survivors. Most of this kind of research has focused on women who remained in the conflict area, were internally displaced, or had fled to refugee camps in neighboring countries. So far knowledge about what the aftermath of the sexual violence experienced in the context of violent conflicts is in terms of health consequences for women who have sought refuge in countries in the West is fairly scanty. In particular, we have very little idea of how these women themselves and others who are in contact with them face the various consequences from the moment they enter such a country until they have gone through the process of settling there. One of the reasons for this lack of knowledge is that sexual violence is an issue which is surrounded by so much taboo, shame, guilt, and fear for loss of family honor for many refugee women that it is difficult for them to talk about it to others, including health-care providers and researchers. In spite of such an apparent lack of progress, some of us have succeeded in gaining some insights into the various kinds of distress suffered by refugee women as a result of the sexual violence they experienced. Reflecting on these insights, we agree completely with the conveners of the EASA conference session "Facing distress: Distance and proximity in times of illness", at which a draft of this paper was presented, that the concepts distance and proximity are "concepts *par excellence* to describe what may happen in times of illness and suffering".

On the basis of four ethnographically informed refugee and violence studies, we will explore how the concepts of distance and proximity can be used to gain a better understanding of what refugee women may go through in the aftermath of sexual violence. All four studies focus, exclusively or in part, on women who escaped from the violent conflict in their country of origin and came to the Netherlands to seek asylum. Included are both women who are in the process of seeking asylum in the Netherlands and women who have an official refugee status in this country[15]. For both groups of women, escape from the violence in their country of origin did not per definition mean that the violence in their life stopped. They may have experienced more sexual and other kinds of violence during their flight, in reception and detention centers in the Netherlands, and, if allowed to remain in this country, subsequently in other living environments. Perpetrators range from strangers, people women have to live with in refugee centers but were previously unknown to them, and husbands or other family members (Kramer & Cense 2004).

Keeping to the specific focus of this book and with reference to the results of the four studies mentioned, the following questions are addressed in this chapter: How do refugee women themselves relate to their distress caused by sexual violence in terms of distance and proximity? To what extent and why do they choose to hide or disclose their experiences related to the sexual violence perpetrated against them in contacts with others? Secondly, how do those others in their turn approach and face up to the distress women suffer from as a consequence of the sexual violence they have experienced in terms of distance and proximity? The "others" referred to in this chapter include legal officials examining women's asylum claims, medical doctors trying to assist sexually abused women in their quest for asylum, health-care workers to whom these women have turned for support and treatment, family members (in particular husbands), other members of the refugee group to which the women belong, and researchers studying refugee women's suffering as a

---

[15] In this chapter the term refugee is used both for forced migrants who have submitted a formal request for asylum and whose request is being examined and for those who obtained the status of "recognized refugee". In the Netherlands, in judicial terms the first category of forced migrants is called asylum seekers. We will use this latter term when the asylum procedure is key to the issue presented.

result of sexual violence and also the way others react to these women and their suffering.

As an introduction to the presentation of the four studies we will briefly present some of the health consequences of sexual violence for women, in particular the psychological consequences as far as they relate to a variety of distance and proximity issues. These issues will be explored more deeply in the particular contexts described in the four case studies. It will be demonstrated how political, legal, economic, social, and cultural variables shape distancing and approximation processes with regard to the sexual violence to which refugee women have been exposed.

## Sexual violence and its health consequences

The concept of sexual violence usually refers to any act of sexual nature which is committed on a person under circumstances which are coercive. Included are not only acts of rape – that is, acts limited to the physical invasion of the human body – but also acts which do not involve penetration or even physical contact. Consequently, sexual violence is often understood to cover a wide range of violent acts of a sexual nature. Examples are individual and mass rape, compulsory nudity, electroshock applied to the nipples and vagina, the squeezing or binding of breasts, suspension of breasts, sexual mutilation, being threatened with the above, forced pregnancy, sexual slavery, forced prostitution, and sex trafficking on a large scale. In the vocabulary of the people concerned, however, sexual violence is often reduced to rape (Tankink 2004). And even then, rape may have a yet more restricted meaning than what is referred to in international documents in which these above definitions are used. For a woman, for instance, who is abducted in a war situation and forced to have sex with her new "husband" who saved her from further abuses, this sex may not be considered as rape (Bel Khodja 2004). It is therefore important to realize that international definitions do not always chime in with the conceptions victims have of the acts referred to in these definitions. Unless stated otherwise, our point of departure is sexual violence as defined in international human rights documents, and women's right to be free from all the kinds of sexual violence which are set out in these documents.

In the context of violent conflicts it is mostly women and children who are targeted by sexual violence. Nevertheless it should not be forgotten that men can also be targets (e.g. Oosterhoff et al. 2004). As the focus of this article is on women, male abuse is beyond its scope.

The health consequences of sexual violence for women can be many. They range from physical health problems (because of HIV/AIDS), gynecological problems (reproductive tract infections, infertility), psycho-somatic complaints (chronic headaches, musculo-skeletal complaints, gastro-intestinal problems), relational problems, fear of social contact resulting in social withdrawal, and major long-term psychological suffering. The last includes anxiety and panic attacks, depression, abuse of medication, alcohol, and drugs, a tendency to suicide, and post-traumatic stress disorder (PTSD).

The characteristic symptoms of PTSD may be threefold: intrusion in the form of re-experiencing of the traumatic event(s) in the form of nightmares and flashbacks; avoidance in the form of a numbed responsiveness to or reduced involvement with the external world; and hyper-alertness or exaggerated startle response. The long-term effects of sexual violence, particularly if this has been one part of multiple traumatic events, include more complex and diffuse symptoms. The women suffering from them may undergo drastic personality changes, particularly relational and identity problems. Herman (2001) uses the term "complex PTSD" for these changes. One of the symptoms of complex PTSD is that the women's basic assumptions are shattered by the chronic traumas they have experienced. These assumptions may include the idea that the world is benevolent, the idea that the world is meaningful, the idea that other people are trustworthy, the idea that I am worthy, the idea that I am in control of my life, and the idea that I am invulnerable (it will not happen to me).

It was the war in the former Yugoslavia especially which boosted the introduction of trauma programs as part of humanitarian interventions in conflict and post-conflict areas around the world. This development stimulated a debate in the literature about the validity of the PTSD concept as point of departure for all these programs. The discourse in the West about violence, loss, and trauma is focused on the long-term effects of what happens inside the body and the psyche. In other cultures various forms of such abuses as torture, including rape, may be perceived not so much as an assault on the "individual self", but more as destruction of family and group relations and a disruption of the moral order. Relational, socio-cultural wounds then have priority over individual wounds, or are at least of equal importance. In such cases we can speak of psycho-socio-cultural trauma, a trauma which besides healing on an individual level requires healing of the post-traumatic stress in the fabrics of culture and society. This raises the question of how individual and socio-cultural post-traumatic stress as well as healing of both kinds of stress relate to each other (Richters 1994).

## Pathways between distance and proximity in the landscape of distress: The influence of contextual factors

In the normal course of coming to terms with the psychological effects of traumatic events, the symptoms of intrusion and avoidance first alternate and slowly fade away. There are many factors which determine the intensity and duration of this process. Important among them are the perception by the victim of the seriousness of the traumatic event, the degree of powerlessness the victim experienced during the event, the amount of preparedness and non-preparedness for the event, the duration of exposure to the event, and the fact whether the victim is affected by just one or by a conglomeration of traumatic events.

What is perceived as having been the most traumatic of all the events to which the person has been exposed may change over time. Hayden (2000: 35) refers to a Bosnian Muslim woman who said during an international conference on Bosnia held in early 1993 that she felt the international emphasis on rape was inappropriate, because all Bosnian women were victims: they lost their homes, their sons, their husbands, their jobs, their lives, and whether they have been sexually assaulted or not was really beside the point. In the Netherlands, social workers who work with female refugees from Bosnia told us that they often hear this same "reproach". In other words, what these women suffer from is "multiple trauma" or "massive trauma", rape being just one element. However, as we will demonstrate later, in due course the rape event(s) may become more prominent in the lives of refugee women in comparison to other traumatic experiences.

A safe and supportive environment after the traumatic event(s) counts highly among the factors which may contribute to a rapid dissipation of the psychological distress or at least to its diminution. Since refugee women have generally experienced sexual violence as part of a conglomerate of serious traumatic events over a longer period of time, they run a far greater risk of developing a complex PTSD and other serious mental health problems. It is only when the post-traumatic stress symptoms continue over time that a condition develops which may be called pathological and may need specialist care.

Whether of short or long duration, the symptoms of intrusion are often so stressful that people suffering from them wish to distance themselves from them and get rid of them altogether by trying to forget what happened to them. Instead they may want to focus, if possible, on putting their life in order again and working towards a better future. Even when forgetting proves impossible, they wish that the memory of the trauma will not burden the present too much. The problem for refugee women is that often there are a number of restraints which make it impossible for them to direct their attention away from their memories and day-to-day problems and involve themselves in new tasks in their immediate environment and in society.

It is not only the immediate psychological distress that inveigles women into forgetting about their ordeal. The culturally colored taboo, shame, and guilt surrounding the subject of sexual violence can be factors which aggravate their distress and the desire not to remember what happened. Under such circumstances, references by others to the sexual violence they have experienced may trigger the trauma of memory again. In other words, delving too close to the experiences of sexual violence of women who are traumatized by them may be an extra source of distress. To encourage healing processes for other purposes, however, it may be in a woman's best interest to disclose some of her experiences. The skill is to judge which is more in a woman's interest, disclosing her experiences by talking about them or silencing them for the sake of her mental health. We will argue below that, while reflecting upon this question, it is crucial to take the particular social and cultural context of a woman's life world into account.

One of the cultural issues which should be borne in mind is that in some cultures women may not have the vocabulary to name a certain experience as sexual violence, coerced sex, or rape. This does not necessarily mean that those women do not feel violated after an event which in international human rights documents would be called sexual violence or rape. Admittedly, through various cultural changes women do learn to speak about certain experiences as rape, but even then they are selective in disclosing those experiences. It may also be that the memories of violent experiences are channeled only through the body and that this body language is the only language that betrays women's pain and suffering inflicted on them by their experiences of violence.

If and how a refugee woman speaks in words about her experiences of sexual violence with another person, and by speaking breaks through her shame and the cultural taboos surrounding sexual violence, depends in part on the context of the encounter with this person and particularly on the attitude of the person facing her. How does the other person relate to the subject of sexual violence experienced by the person facing him or her in terms of distance and proximity? And how does he or she relate to cultural differences? Does he or she succeed in creating an atmosphere in which the woman in question feels secure enough to disclose (some of) her experiences? These and related issues will be discussed with reference to encounters refugee women have with others in the course of legal procedures, medical examinations, surviving in their day-to-day life, therapy, and research.

The main focus of the next sections is on the facing of their distress by refugee women themselves and others in the Netherlands, and less on the facing of the distress in the country of origin where the sexual violence took place, even though for the women concerned both are related. We will start with the distress refugee women and others face during the asylum procedure. From there we will proceed to refugee women's distress in day-to-day life. We will end with the distress faced in the professional treatment of refugee women who have lived in the Netherlands for some time. In the discussion we will elaborate on the distress generated by anthropological field research on sexual violence and related issues of distance and proximity.

## Seeking refuge from war and sexual violence: Distance and proximity in legal hearings

The Netherlands has had one of the most restrictive asylum practices in Europe since the implementation of a new refugee determination procedure in 2001. Despite the fact that people seeking asylum often enter the country where they hope to find safety in bad physical and mental shape, on arrival in the Netherlands the majority of them have to prove their case within a period of 48 working hours after arrival. On the basis of the first interview upon entry at an "application center", conducted by officers of the Ministry of Justice, the decision is made whether or not the asylum seeker will be accepted into the full refugee determination procedure. Should they be accepted, a further hearing at an office of the Immigration and Naturalization Service (IND) is the only opportunity given the asylum seeker to put forward the motives for his or her flight. This hearing usually takes place within a month of the refugee's arrival. If the further hearing leads to a negative decision, it is possible to lodge an appeal with the help of a lawyer.

In 2002, in her capacity as a volunteer social legal worker, Bel Khodja accompanied and assisted asylum seekers during further hearings. In doing so she assumed a double role. As an anthropologist she observed what happened during the hearings she attended. Her special interest focused on the stories of women who had experienced sexual violence and the way these stories were listened to by IND officials.

Women survivors who have fled political violence in their countries of origin and hope to receive protection in the Netherlands are seldom sufficiently informed about asylum proceedings or of the importance of the IND interviews in the determination process. They may not realize, for instance, that under certain conditions sexual violence can be accepted as a reason for granting refugee status on humanitarian grounds. The "further hearing" in the asylum procedure is often the first time and place in which they are asked "what happened". The violence-related distress coupled with the distancing tactics adopted by the interviewing officials may prevent women from answering this question appropriately or even answering it at all. The paradox is that the IND creates a large distance between itself and refugees but at the same time expects that they will reveal things which can only be said in an atmosphere of proximity and trust.

Bel Khodja (2004) describes the further hearings as ritualistic performances. The goals of such a performance are not so much to find out who needs protection and grant it, but to perform the magic juggling task of rejecting 80% of asylum claims but preserving the self-image of a people imbued with the necessity of helping others in need and distress. The further hearings attended by Bel Khodja were usually held in an atmosphere devoid of emotion but "correct". Nine of the twelve women whom Bel Khodja accompanied to their hearing reported rape violence and/or other forms of sexual violence as a reason for their flight. Ten women had given her permission to tell their stories anonymously, which she did in her thesis (2004). The researcher found that the distress which these women experienced during the refugee status determination interviews was often either not recognized or misinterpreted by interviewing officials. These are often so obsessed with unmasking potential "bogus" refugees, that they perceive the distress of the women as a good reason to doubt their credibility. The upshot of this attitude is that distressed women do not receive the care they deserve and are not offered any of the medical assistance to which they are entitled.

All the refugees Bel Khodja accompanied were asked during their hearing whether they had experienced sexual violence. This question was posed as a standard question at the end of the interview. The women were sometimes asked to give a detailed description of rape violence. The officials interviewing never told them during such interviews that they could refuse to answer a question, which is an absolute prerequisite in questioning about rape violence. The officials who carried out the first two hearings Bel Khodja describes in her thesis were blatantly unfriendly, especially when they were questioning the women about experiences of sexual violence. They both seemed obsessed with the task of proving refugees liars and their harshness when asking interviewees about human rights abuses was downright cruel.

Anna B. was nineteen years of age when she fled her country of birth, Sierra Leone. Although she had already recounted her gang rape and abduction by rebels, she was not offered a female interpreter. The male interpreter assumed an arrogant attitude. It was usual for him to receive telephone calls during interviews, and he had refused to desist. He also took great pleasure in ridiculing refugees, which he proceeded to do during Anna's 'hearing'. When Anna began to tell her personal story, both the official interviewing her and the interpreter seemed totally uninterested.

"The rebels came into the house. ... One of the rebels ... wanted sex with me. I did not want to. I was pregnant. I fought with him, but he beat me with his weapon and raped me. Then he went outside. Another came in. Five rebels raped me and I lost a lot of blood. ... The commander of the group ... picked me up and took me with him. ... He used me as his wife. ...". After Anna B. had told this story, she was upset, but was unable to cry.

What is characteristic of Anna's "narrative of rape violence" is that she considers only gang rape, rape violence. She is unable to recognize the rape by the man who abducted her as rape. Calling the relationship between slave and slave master marriage legitimizes rape in Sierra Leone.

Anna was illiterate. She did not know the names of rivers in Sierra Leone and, when she was asked about the rainy season, she said that she did not know the names of the months. The interpreter started to laugh and, after he translated Anna's answer, both interviewing official and interpreter seemed smug and self-congratulatory. It was obvious that they considered Anna's answer proof that she was lying.

On the basis of her observations, Bel Khodja confirms what the student anthropologist Groot (1999) found in her anthropological research at an IND office. The interviewing officials consider refugees' stories believable for just as long as they can identify with them. The further the context of their narrative is removed from the Dutch context, the harder they find it to empathize. One of Groot's informants in the IND service said: "You can deal with some cultures more easily than others. I think in my case Africa is the most difficult, just because people are so far removed from us. ... It is so much more difficult to relate to what is happening in Rwanda [than in the former Yugoslavia]. It is more difficult to empathize with these peoples' lives". (ibid.: 74)

In Anna B's case, the interpreter and interviewing official continued to talk and laugh in the smoking area after the interview, pointedly looking at the legal aid worker, in this case the anthropologist, and Anna B. sitting in the waiting-room.

A second harrowing case is that of Phyllis C., a sixteen-year-old girl from Nigeria. Bel Khodja found Phyllis curled up in a fetal position in one of the plastic chairs in the waiting-room area of the IND office. During the hearing, the louder Phyllis cried when asked about details of her experiences of sexual violence, the more unfriendly the young female interviewing official became. Phyllis was totally exhausted at the end of her "hearing". A few days later Bel Khodja received a telephone call and was told that Phyllis C. had disappeared from the reception centre for asylum seekers on her way to the medical office in this centre. Phyllis C. was not an exception.

For anthropologists the ethical and epistemological question is what position they should adopt in such a field as that described above? Bel Khodja commenced her fieldwork with a passion for the subject of her study. In order to overcome the dehumanization she encountered in the IND offices, she moved beyond the "theatrical frame" and became intensely involved with the refugee women she assisted during her fieldwork, sharing their pain and their tears. Her relationship with them was often impeded by fear of over-involvement and a dread of becoming emotionally overwhelmed. These fears were nurtured by thoughts of "professionalism", which values professional distance more than professional involvement. Bel Khodja struggled to find the right balance between this involvement and the professional distance also required of an anthropologist.

Bel Khodja's ethical reflection with regard to the IND interview process is that, if the interview question about what happened is not posed with honest interest, a ready ear, and some compassion for the pain experienced, it should not be asked at all. It should be realized, however, that sexual violence may be taken into consideration as a reason for being granted asylum, so it also seems to be in a woman's best interest that she speak about it in hearings about her asylum petition. The problem is that international guidelines state that a woman should only be invited to do so if the condition of her health is taken into consideration and she is receiving the health care she needs. Women should also be made aware of their right to refuse to answer a question, stop an interview, and to be interviewed by a female interviewer. The onus is on the IND interviewer to safeguard that right. Quite apart from this, the interviewer – just as a health-care worker and a researcher – should be able to judge whether it is justified to confront a particular woman with her past experiences given her distressed condition, to recognize signs of re-traumatization, and to know how to act in a woman's best interest should re-traumatization take place.

### A further search for evidence: Distance and proximity in medical examination processes

Bel Khodja's study confirms observations made in other studies and in many media reports claiming that a refugee's best interest is generally not a priority of IND officials. This is different in the medical examination processes conducted by physicians who work for the Medical Examination Group of Amnesty International (AI) on a voluntary basis.

Asylum seekers whose request for asylum is denied are entitled to ask Amnesty International to support the documentation of their asylum petition by a medical examination through the intervention of a solicitor. This is not a step in the appeal process favored by IND. IND rules stipulate that a recourse to medical expertise is not part of the asylum procedures. In fact, IND instructions state that: "Medical examination cannot contribute to verification" (Bruin 2001). The consequence of this perspective is that medical information can be kept completely invisible, even in the reports of the State-financed Medical Services associated with asylum facilities. Only in an appeal stage, and usually following several negative decisions, at the request of a defense solicitor, can a medical report be produced and shown to the judge of appeal, who may accept it and order the IND to re-conduct its hearing and/or reconsider its decision (even the judge cannot reverse the IND decision).

The IND conception of medical documentation is completely at odds with the Human Rights Acts and their medical implications as demonstrated in, for instance, the Istanbul Protocol (2001). The upshot of this conflict in interpretation is that AI has instituted a corps of approximately 25 Dutch medical volunteers trained in the appropriate medical examinations. Since 1977, more than 5000 reports have been produced. Recently the annual production has been approximately 100. It is the ambition of AI to play a role in ensuring that the misrepresentation of the asylum seeker's story by IND is stopped and reversed should torture (including sexual violence) be the event which prompted the request for asylum.

Oomen is one of the medical doctors who have worked for more than ten years for the AI Medical Examination Group (MEG). As part of his recent MA study in medical anthropology, he made a retrospective analysis of his

Amnesty work on the basis of a review of the medical examinations he himself had conducted and a number of interviews with experts in the field of refugee issues. Oomen (2004) claims that listening to refugees' stories as a medical examiner requires not only empathy (proximity), but, for the sake of verification of the medical evidence provided by the asylum seeker, also impartiality, problematizing what is told and contextualizing it (distance). A psychiatrist who also works for MEG, emphasized when she was interviewed by Oomen the proximity aspects of the medical examination. She believes that the most rewarding approach to the asylum seeker is to invest in an environment of safety, positive contact, mutual trust, emotional comfort, and empathy. The medical intervention is often experienced by the asylum seeker as a final station, at the end of a journey which has drained all his or her resources. This may partly explain why clients who did not disclose their experiences of sexual violence during the IND hearings will reveal those experiences during an Amnesty examination.

Many more men than women seek help from Amnesty. This can be explained by the fact that men dominate the influx of refugees in Western countries; the male-female ratio is roughly 3:1. Both men and women report sexual abuse frequently, but women more often than men. In a representative sample of 157 MEG reports produced in the period 1998-1999, 73% of women and 32% of men reported having suffered from sexual violence. Out of the 30 clients examined by Oomen in the period 1994-2004, 24 were men and 6 were women. Seven of the 24 men reported a history of sexual assault, and all women reported such a history. Five of the 6 women talked about sexual violence in the form of rape. In comparison to others, who had not endured sexual assaults, clients who had been raped suffered complaints which emphasized the combination of physical (for example, constipation, vaginal discomfort, menstrual disorders), sexual (impotence, infertility, loss of libido), and psychiatric complaints (Oomen 2004).

Amnesty examinations reveal that cultural factors or mental or physical discomfort have prevented victims of sexual violence disclosing the traumatic event during IND hearings or to family members and friends. This happened to a 30-year-old female from the Sudan, Sarah B., who had, in her country of origin, been abducted, raped, and beaten by two unknown perpetrators. Her guilt and shame were so great she was incapable of admitting the trauma to her relatives. Instead she made up a story of harassment by state officials. Her family helped her to escape to her husband, who had obtained refugee status in the Netherlands. In the first asylum hearing, she kept the rape secret for fear that her husband, now her only support, would reject her. After receiving a negative decision by IND, Sarah discussed the real trauma to her Refugee Council contact and was advised to disclose the rape in a second procedure. Unfortunately, because of the intervention, her husband became aware of it and did indeed reject her. In the asylum appeal, the court ruled that she should have disclosed the actual trauma in the first round of hearings and, having failed to do so, the negative decision was not overturned. Her solicitor appealed with the help of Amnesty International and her case is still awaiting a final judgment.

Before and during the medical examination by Amnesty, Sarah informed the female psychiatrist supporting and treating her that she was not willing to testify to the rape she had endured, even if the interpreter was a woman. She saw the interpreter as a representative of her own social environment and feared her disapproval. Sarah was certain that she would be expelled from her community once her rape trauma was made known to others of the same background. Subsequently the psychiatrist found out that, not only had she not testified to it before, but also that she had in fact no words or metaphors to describe for what had happened to her. According to the psychiatrist that inability to express herself about her experiences of sexual violence requires: both (a) well-directed treatment to overcome her silence, and (b) training in giving testimony the same way a professional would, that is in a proto-professionalized manner.

At issue is whether, in their treatment of female clients during an appeal process, other psychiatrists share the view of this particular psychiatrist. As we will indicate later, health-care providers specialized in treating women with a history of sexual abuse, including refugee women, are, with good reason, very careful about encouraging the disclosure of the sexual abuse and may decide not to do so at all. The individual need for secrecy and the social request for disclosure cause a conflict, which requires inventiveness to overcome. The important lesson in Oomen's retrospective study is that Human Rights Acts are rights, which do not act. The government can get away with denial, even blatant refusal to look at the medical evidence, when to do so is politically profitable and the victims lack any possibility to overcome their fear for disclosure.

## Agency under cultural censorship: Distance and proximity in day-to-day-life

Sarah's story as presented above reveals a refugee woman's fear of disclosing experiences of sexual violence to members of the refugee community to which she belongs. How deeply this fear is rooted was experienced by Tankink in her anthropological study of the meaning refugee women in the Netherlands give to the sexual violence they have experienced.

Tankink's study focuses on refugee women from Afghanistan, Bosnia, and South Sudan and is still ongoing (Tankink 2004). As a community psychiatric nurse with a ten-year-long experience in the care of women with a history of sexual abuse, Tankink has learned how to develop the necessary trust relationship with these women, how to respect their silence, and how to react to disclosure and its possible negative effects on the health of the woman as a consequence. Even for her in her position, however, it proved to be very difficult and time consuming to get access to refugee women who had themselves experienced sexual violence and who were willing to talk about their experiences. Tankink has been trying to get this access via organized refugee groups and the snowball effect, thereby anticipating that cultural taboos, fear, pain, and shame would make it difficult to discuss the experiences and the consequences of sexual violence with the women. For almost twelve months it turned out to be nigh on impossible to find women who were willing to talk about their experiences of sexual violence – which for them is often a synonym for rape – and nobody dared to give the names of other women whom they thought may have experienced sexual violence. Gradually, however, some women did come forward with their experiences. Of the 46 women Tankink interviewed, seventeen revealed experiences of sexual violence and one woman told about the rape of her daughter. It was remarkable that these eighteen women all opened up to her at the very first meeting.

A preliminary analysis of the research findings thus far supports the interpretation of the individual and communal forms of silence surrounding sexual violence as cultural censorship (Sheriff 2000). Sheriff argues that that although "...there may be meaningful, even profound, psychological motivations underlying this silence, it is socially shared; the rules for its observance are culturally codified" (ibid.: 114). Approvingly, Sheriff (ibid. 117) refers to Saunders' analysis of silence among the Italian families he studied. Drawing on the anthropology of emotions, Saunders (1985:175) writes that: "...silence may be an indication of conflicting or problematic emotions, emotions which must be monitored, controlled, or inhibited in expression because of their political consequences". This does not mean that cultural censorship precludes agency. It assuredly does involve a degree of agency, "...for it is a 'form of forgetting', or more precisely, it is a practice that is directed toward 'trying not to remember'" (Sheriff 2000:122).

The refugee women in Tankink's study who prefer silence to disclosure do so because of fear for expulsion from their family and/or refugee community. Some women are able to reveal their experiences of sexual violence to their sister or mother, knowing that they will keep silent. All refugee women who lack the emotional support and protection of their own relatives in the Netherlands are dependent on the refugee group they belong to for support and social contacts. Although the various refugee groups have taken over some functions which are normally performed by relatives – such as attending to weddings, celebrations, and funerals – the group members will not, in contrast to the sisters or mothers of the women concerned, keep silent when aspects of honor and shame are involved.

All Afghan women said that it would be better to commit suicide than to make their experiences of sexual violence known. Although the Bosnian and South Sudanese women do not think that it would be better for a raped woman to kill herself, just as the Afghan women they fear social death within the refugee ethnic group to which they belong. Social "death" does not per definition mean physical exclusion by the group, but loss of honor and strong disapproval, directly and indirectly, which often has an extremely negative effect on the self-esteem of the women involved.

All the women interviewed by Tankink are extremely anxious about gossip in which a woman might be accused of having broken the cultural code of preserving her sexual integrity, her identity, and her honor as a woman. This all results in a very isolated position for women, because they have nobody with whom to share their problems. Noria C., an Afghan mother whose daughter was raped, has broken all her contacts with Afghan people in the Netherlands. She does not want to lie; therefore she thinks it is better for her to avoid any contact. She hopes she can keep the fact that her daughter has lost her sexual integrity secret and thus can retain her own honor because, as a mother, Noria is responsible for the upbringing of her children and she fears being accused of having failed dramatically. In Noria's case a fully cognizant silence is experienced as a realistic and "adaptive" response to domination.

Women are placed in the situation that they are judged according to cultural notions of femininity and gender roles which they want to cast off, but they are none the less ruled still by them. This cultural censorship has been internalized at a conscious and unconscious level. In Noria's eyes it is normal: "It is my culture", she often says. The judgments of members of the particular refugee group to which a woman belongs are often revealed also in gossip.

Gossiping is, according to the women, rifer than it was in their country of origin. People have no history together, except for the history of being refugees from the same country. They neither know nor trust each other. Gossiping is a way of getting more information about other persons; it creates proximity. Furthermore, gossiping helps them to keep their personal problems at a distance because they are concentrated on the other. In creating a sense of belonging to a group, gossip can have a positive function. At the same time, however, gossip can also be damaging to the individual; it can destroy a person's identity, honor, and dignity. Gossip creates distance and the fear of negative rumors can make women decide to break off contacts with other compatriots. Silence stemming from cultural censorship is strongly connected with proximity and distance. Not talking about sexual violence means relinquishing social support on this issue, but keeping silent is a prerequisite for getting social support on other, less sensitive issues. In other words it creates distance and proximity at the same time in different realms of experiences.

It is very likely that the need for professional help may strengthen in situations where women cannot find support. In the Netherlands, a woman who needs psychological help has to go to her family doctor, who can refer the woman involved, if necessary according his or her diagnosis, to a specialist. Many women are, however, dissatisfied with their family doctor. Their complaints are too easily labeled stress and it is rare for any serious investigation to take place. This might be partly attributable to the fact that general practitioners make hardly any use of the professional interpreters available via the telephone. Therefore the communication is poor. The refugee women cannot speak about their experiences if relatives or friends are translating, afraid of the consequences if the latter should discover their secret. It seems that without the intervention of Dutch friends, family doctors do not easily refer women to specialists in mental health or gynecology.

As an anthropologist doing research on sexual violence, Tankink herself also struggles with distance and proximity, albeit of a different kind. The appalling stories of the women, including those who did not disclose their own sexual experiences or perhaps did not suffer them, often create simultaneous feelings of proximity and powerlessness, while the role as researcher also requires distance in order to be able to look at the stories at another level. Whereas in the first period of her research Tankink began to worry that her questions were too difficult for the women, in the sense that all the memories and the feelings of pain resurfaced, she now realizes that for many women the possibility to talk in a strictly confidential setting besides eliciting the feelings of pain and shame, also brings some feelings of relief.

## Healing of trauma: Distance and proximity in professional therapy

Eventually some refugee women do find their way to care providers who are specialized in refugee mental health. This does not automatically mean that their experiences of sexual violence are disclosed in therapy sessions. How health-care providers do approach the issue of sexual violence in terms of distance and proximity was revealed to some extent in a study by Cense (2002).

Cense realized beforehand that, because talking about sexual violence can arouse feelings of shame, anxiety, and guilt provoked by the remembering of the sexual violence (again), the first essential is to create a trust relationship before starting to interview women about their experiences of sexual violence. Given the restricted time she had for the research she wanted to do and not being a health-care provider herself, she felt that it was out of the question for her to create that trust relationship. She therefore decided to approach the subject of her interest through interviews with health-care providers.

Cense's main research methods consisted of interviewing five health-care providers experienced in providing mental health care for refugee and migrant women with experiences of sexual violence. All five therapists were very emotionally involved with their clients and without exception talked with great passion about the issues at stake in the care of clients with different cultural backgrounds. Consequently, indirectly, the research succeeded in coming close to the distress of women who had experienced sexual violence, to the meaning they gave to this distress, and to healing processes.

The clients of whom the mental health-care providers spoke in their interview with Cense had been referred to them, for instance, by general practitioners. Depending on the reason given for the referral, the therapist decided whether or not to address the issue of sexual violence immediately during the first therapy session. It might take many sessions before the issue of sexual violence is directly addressed, even though the therapist is almost sure that the client's suffering can be attributed to the sexual violence she experienced. The situation may also arise in which the client knows that the therapist knows she has experienced sexual violence, but that the experience is never named and openly discussed. Also, when women in group sessions know that each of them has experienced sexual violence, the secrecy around the issue may never be lifted. It may also be that the experience is discussed only in very indirect terms, using plenty of symbolic speech (Kirmayer 2000), speaking of "no longer being a young flower", or using only the language of the body. Although not openly speaking about the sexual violence, the client may be able to give indications of the necessity to perform particular rituals or of the need for other forms of sociality to diminish her suffering.

There may therefore be a very empathic relationship between client and therapist, understanding each other very well, being aware that the experiences of sexual violence are present all the time, while both distance themselves from talking about it. At a certain point the therapist has to make the difficult decision about whether the disclosure of the secret will be tolerable to the client and what kind of therapy should be preferred. Should she as a therapist, for instance, involve family members: yes or no?

Issues raised by Cense's study are: If and to what extent is the appropriation of rape trauma healthier than distancing from that trauma for the individual woman? Is it possible that the distance from the collectivity of the refugee group in therapy rooms and the benevolent image therapists present may enable individuals to borrow helpful, new elements to come closer to the trauma so as to begin the process of psychological healing, while remaining in contact with their group of origin (Atlani & Rousseau 2000)? Or, would it be better for the health of the victim, in this case the client, for the silence to be respected throughout the therapy, because acceptance by the community is seen by the client as her priority? Or should the client's desire to forget be supported in therapy because the woman wants to be able to focus on rebuilding her life instead of digging into the traumatic memories of the past? In the practice of therapy, answers to these questions may be different in each particular case, depending on such factors as the severity of the mental health problems and the nature of the living environment of the women concerned.

One issue not addressed by Cense is the dilemma with which mental health professionals may be faced in their treatment of asylum seekers. What should be done when they are of the opinion that pressuring the client to disclose their experiences of sexual violence may be damaging to their mental health status, while simultaneously talking about the experiences may be in the direct interest of the client if she is involved in a refugee status hearing or medical examination? The psychiatrist who consulted in the Amnesty case of Sarah discussed above did not see any dilemma here, but other psychiatrists may well have a different experience when a client admits to them that they have a history of sexual abuse but that they explicitly do not want to testify about it to others.

## Concluding remarks

Sexual violence is a traumatic event in the lives of many refugee women which usually causes them various kinds of psychological distress. The level and kind of distress are closely related to various cultural and social factors, as has been demonstrated above. A safe and supportive environment – whether in an office of IND, Amnesty International, or a mental health-care therapist, in interviews with a researcher, or in day-to-day life – can help to find the right balance between the approximation and distancing of the event in memories and stories. In order to find meaning in life again, it is essential sociality be maintained or restored. Previous kinds of sociality may have been destroyed, so consequently new ones have to be created. Sociality, even if a traumatized one, may be experienced by refugee women as more important to their survival than disclosing their traumatic experiences for the sake of obtaining justice. The dilemma is that justice may help the recovery process. Therefore, everything in the intrapersonal and interpersonal realm has to be done to optimize the interaction processes essential to the awarding of a justified refugee status.

Besides the refugee women themselves and the members of the refugee groups to which these women belong, the main actors in this chapter have been IND officials, medical doctors working for Amnesty International, professional mental health-care workers, and researchers. It became clear that for all these professional groups it is important to know what women suffering from (post)traumatic distress go through psychologically, how contextual factors can contribute to their distress or its relief, and how one as an individual professional or as a group of professionals can have a positive or negative impact on the distress, either directly or by influencing other relevant contextual factors. Anthropologists may be able to explain to other professionals how cultural censorship operates and the various ways refugee women relate to it. They may also contribute to knowledge of healing processes in other cultural contexts, for instance, the healing in group processes as they take place in post-conflict societies in Africa. An example is the healing in a group of women who, knowing that each other was raped, cook, sing, cry, listen to each others' stories and dance together. However, it may take many more strenuous efforts to form such a group among refugee women in the Netherlands because of feelings of insecurity and distrust, or because of the women's social environments which raise many barriers to disclosure. Besides, because of the veil of silence drawn over the issue, refugee women in the Netherlands seldom know other women who have experienced sexual violence. Tankink's research confirms that women feel a strong need to keep silent but also feel great relief after they had dared to disclose their stories to the researcher. For health-care workers this could mean that they have to respect a woman's wish to keep her rape trauma secret and that it can be helpful to discuss the background to this wish in therapy. In addition, it might be very helpful for women to know that therapy can offer them a private, safe environment in which to talk about traumatic experiences without being forced to reveal those experiences to the environment in which they live. Conversely, the therapist may judge it relevant to a particular client to inform at least one person in her immediate environment about the rape trauma in order to win the support of this person.

As researchers, anthropologists in their turn can learn from psychiatry what are the usual symptoms of post-traumatic stress and the caution to be observed in talking to refugee women about their past and present experiences of traumatic events. More and more anthropological research is taking place in populations which have been exposed to violent conflicts. In these situations, the application of the customary approaches, methods, and ethics of anthropological fieldwork may be insufficient, irrelevant, inapplicable, imprudent, or simply naïve. What are needed are updated field strategies for dealing with the well-being of informants exposed to violence as well as for anthropologists who work with them. Anthropologists will also have to learn the art of balancing between distance and proximity while facing their own distress generated by being confronted with the distress of such others as refugee women suffering mental and physical anguish as a result of their traumatization by experiences of sexual violence.

## References

Atlani, L. & Rousseau, C.

2000 The politics of culture in humanitarian aid to women refugees who have experienced sexual violence. *Transcultural Psychiatry* 37, 3: 435-449.

Bel Khodja, H.

2004 *"Give me your ears!" Seeking refuge from sexual violence: Further hearings in the Netherlands*. MA thesis Cultural Anthropology, University of Amsterdam.

Bruin, R. (ed.)

2001 *Wederzijds Wantrouwen*. Giethoorn: Ten Brink.

Cense, M.

2002 *Door nieuwe ogen: Betekenisgeving en hulp na seksueel geweld in cultureel perspectief*. MA thesis Interculturalisation of Care, Utrecht University.

Groot, C.

1999 *De poortwachters van Nederland: Over ambtenaren en de asielprocedure*. MA thesis Cultural Anthropology. University of Amsterdam.

Hayden, R.M.

2000 Rape and rape avoidance in ethno-national conflicts: Sexual violence in liminalized states. *American Anthropologist* 102, 1: 27-42.

Herman, J. L.

2001 [1992] *Trauma and recovery. From domestic abuse to political terror*. London: Pandora.

Istanbul Protocol

2001 *Manual on effective investigation and documentation of torture and other cruel, inhuman or degrading treatment or punishment*. Geneva.

Kirmayer, L.

2000 Broken narratives: Clinical encounters and the poetics of illness experience. In: C. Mattingly & L. Garro (eds.) *Narrative and the cultural con-*

*struction of illness and healing*. Berkeley: University of California Press, pp. 153-181.

Kramer, S. & Cense, M.
2004 *Overleven op de M2: Veiligheidsbeleving en strategieën van vrouwen in de centrale opvang voor asielzoekers*. Utrecht: Pharos, Transact.

Oomen, J.
2004 *Torture narratives and the burden of giving evidence*. MA thesis Medical Anthropology, University of Amsterdam.

Oosterhoff, P.; Zwanikken, P. Ketting, E.
2004 Sexual torture of men in Croatia and other conflict situations: An open secret. *Reproductive Health Matters* 12, 1: 68-78.

Richters, A.
1994 *Women, culture and violence: A development, health and human rights issue*. Leiden: VENA.

Saunders, G.
1985 Silence and noise as emotion management styles: An Italian case. In D. Tannen & M. Saville-Troike (eds.) *Perspectives on silence*. Norwood, NJ: Ablex Publishing Corp., pp. 165-184.

Sheriff, R. E.
2000 Exposing silence as cultural censorship: A Brazilian case. *American Anthropologist* 102, 1: 114-132.

Tankink, M.
2004 *The impact of cultural master narratives on health and coping strategies of refugee women in the Netherlands who experienced sexual violence*. Paper presented at the symposium "Violence, health and human rights: Challenges for medical anthropology". University of Amsterdam.

## Working towards proximity

Charlotte Bredahl Jacobsen

### Introduction

In Danish forensic psychiatry, proximity is an ideal that nursing staff work towards. There are two reasons for this: first, close relationships are goals in themselves and a measure for the success of the treatment; secondly, the knowledge staff need in order to treat a patient is achieved by establishing a close relationship with him. Proximity is an aspiration, but it is also a tool used in and achieved through strategic role play. In this article, I show how proximity, as both an aspiration and a tool, is linked to two partly opposing and yet interlinked approaches that psychiatric nursing staff operate with. I argue that, in working with proximity, psychiatric nursing staff seem to be caught in a paradox. On the one hand they understand proximity as a kind of intersubjectivity that is "true" and they are driven by a quest for it, but on the other hand they see this intersubjectivity as opposed to and challenged by strategic role playing that patients are believed to resort to all too often, yet that they themselves like to explain as something they play as part of their job.

As a path towards understanding the above paradox, I shall illuminate the emic concepts of proximity in use locally and show how these concepts are constructed and dealt with in the interplay between patients and nursing staff. In order to do this, I shall introduce two individuals to act as case studies in this context: Jakob and Ali. Both are patients whom I have engaged in many conversations and have followed over a long period of time. As a patient, Jakob is quiet and calm, but Ali creates or becomes involved in conflicts all the time. Jakob seldom talks about his illness and tries not to let it show in the ward. From time to time Ali is openly psychotic and struggles with strange thoughts that he then wishes to share with everyone. Despite their differences, the two patients have something in common: they are both struggling to find a balance between proximity and distance in their relationship with the staff that satisfies them as well as the staff. Hence, while serving to illustrate the paradox in the staff working towards proximity, the two cases simultaneously show how the close relationship is created under circumstances that may involve painful negotiations and difficult forms of interplay. Their stories tell us of approaches and perceptions, but also what it is like to get caught up in a situation in which the staff demand a certain kind of close relationship that patients may not be able to understand, master or indeed desire.

Data for this analysis come from ten months of fieldwork in locked forensic wards in a psychiatric hospital situated outside Copenhagen, where I studied the interplay between patients and nursing staff. I obtained my material through daily participant observation in the wards, participation in staff meetings and treatment conferences, and formal and informal conversations with staff and patients. I supplemented these data with qualitative interviews.

Since working towards proximity takes place in a context that enables and forms it, I shall start by presenting that context.

## A special context for working towards proximity

Forensic psychiatric wards are a relatively new phenomenon in Denmark. They are the outcome of decisions taken at individual hospitals, where the management team has seen advantages in separating forensic patients, who are typically hospitalised for long periods (often for years), from ordinary psychiatric patients, who may be hospitalised for weeks only. When someone is sentenced to psychiatric treatment in Denmark, he or she may in principle be treated by any psychiatric hospital, as no distinction is made in the law (Poulsen et al. 2000). As regards treatment, this is basically of the same kind that is provided in forensic and ordinary wards (that is, psychopharmacological treatment supplied with milieu therapy in a closed, transparent and structured environment).

The three locked forensic wards I have been in each contain between ten and thirteen beds, mainly in single rooms, and are staffed by three to five members of the nursing staff at all times of the day or night. These staff are trained in nursing or have a Danish two-year certificate of education in care. Psychiatrists, psychologists and social workers are affiliated to each ward.

Psychiatric nursing staff are trained in a combination of phenomenological and psychodynamic approaches to nursing, as taught by Hummelvold (1982), Martinsen (2003) and Strand (1994). With this as their theoretical background, they work reflectively and professionally with the concepts of "distance" and "proximity". They work with proximity on the basis of the idea that this is essential for a total form of care that heals physical as well as mental wounds (Dahlberg 1996). They also work with proximity in order to gain knowledge. Besides the work of care, psychiatric nursing staff are expected to provide the psychiatrist with information that may enable him to determine how ill the patient is and how best to provide him with the appropriate treatment and care. Furthermore, staff should also evaluate and judge the level of control under which the patient should live. Together with the psychiatrist, they evaluate whether the treatment is having an effect, whether the patient is potentially dangerous, whether he is likely to escape if he is allowed outside the locked ward, and whether he is ready for a bed in an open ward. For this they need knowledge, which they acquire by getting to know the patient through a relationship of proximity.

However, staff are put in a difficult situation by the circumstances under which they have to work. Patients are sentenced to treatment – they ask for neither treatment nor close relationships. Besides, the staff trying to create these relationships are precisely the people who keep them locked up.

When a patient is hospitalised, he is often hostile and keeps his distance from the staff. But, as staff explained to me, they are fortunate enough to have plenty of time at their disposal. They therefore keep their distance, but show that they are available by their physical presence. They may sit with a cup of coffee or a news magazine in the living room and wait for the patient to seek contact. They know that at some time the patient will do this, for in this environment everything is locked up. If the patient needs a bath, he has to come and ask the staff for a towel; if he wants to buy sweets or cigarettes, he has to come and ask the staff to help him. Staff have to unlock the door when he wants to wash his clothes, shave, etc. The patient sooner or later realises that he has to contact the staff, and the latter consciously make use of this fact to make the patient himself initiate contact. When the patient does so, staff make sure to be very helpful and friendly. This, they know, is their first step in achieving proximity, and it is important.

Patients learn that the handing out of towels is an important act of communication, and once it is learned they use it as well. Thus I have seen patients resume contact with staff after a conflict by asking them for a towel. There were also ways of bending this communication path, one patient explained to me. When he felt that the staff were not caring about him, he consciously made himself a nuisance to them by asking for towels three or four times a day.

Patients may, of course, obstruct the process of working towards proximity for some time, but they seldom do so forever. Over time, patients learn that a certain level of proximity with staff is a necessity if they want to "get through the system". This expression refers to the way a patient passes from the locked ward to the open ward, and is gradually allowed to move more and more into the public space until he is finally discharged. If a patient has committed a serious crime, staff do not let him through the system before they feel they know him well enough, have become close enough to him, and have the feeling that what they are seeing is the real person. The central part that proximity plays in this treatment process will be investigated further below.

To summarize this section, the restrictive physical environment, its structure, its rules and the circumstances under which patients are hospitalised provide a framework that staff use reflectively in a conscious and strategic process of working towards proximity. In this sense control becomes a means of achieving closeness.

## Control and knowing

It has been argued that acquiring intimate knowledge about a subject is a means of controlling that subject. According to Foucault, a thorough knowledge of the human being is also a requirement for the effective disciplining of the subject. Biographical knowledge of the subject's life and self is a central technique for correcting it (1995: 252). From this perspective, the link between closeness and control is actually the reverse of what I have argued above. It is not my intention to reject the link that Foucault and others have pointed to here – control and knowledge certainly have a dual and reciprocal relationship in forensic psychiatry. However, as will become clear in this chapter, it is rather the idea of "knowing", not actual intimate knowledge, which seems to play a central role in the negotiations over control that take place in the forensic wards in this study. This has to do with the culturally specific ideas about knowing that are current in this Danish institution. Contrary to what one might expect, "knowing" is not a matter of knowing a lot of facts about a patient. Most patients have long case records, but when staff seek to get to know a patient, they seldom read them, or they read a part, only to forget it again. The reason is that knowing is not about knowing facts, but about obtaining a certain feeling. As Anderson describes it from her work in a class in a Danish school, "knowing" implies a certain approach between two people obtained through having seen each other in social interplay. "To know" determines access to others. It opens doors to physical and social closeness, while at the same time this is the place where it is produced (Anderson 2000). From a study of pedagogical work with vulnerable children, Andersen similarly describes how staff refrained from asking the children about their problems. Instead, they felt they could get to know the children through the meta-communication taking place around social activities (Andersen 2003: 141). The meaning of "knowing" in forensic psychiatry seems to accord with the meaning it is ascribed in these other Danish welfare institutions. "Knowing" becomes a central foundation of knowledge which rests on feelings, and thus the central task in getting to know a patient is to acquire something on basis of which one may acquire such feelings (Mik-Meyer 2003: 95). In this way, knowing ends up as something rather indefinable, but it is exactly for this reason that it becomes such a powerful term, and thus a pawn in the game of control. This will become clearer when we turn to the cases of Jakob and Ali later.

## An emic understanding of proximity

Though proximity is a professional term for nursing staff, this does not imply that working with proximity can be understood by reading text books alone. It is important to investigate how proximity as a concept is perceived and created and made central to care in terms of praxis as well.

Proximity is a broad term. What is it to be near someone? The local understanding of this can be explored by paying attention to the metaphoric essence of the emic terms that staff use. In the following I shall first describe the emic term "good contact". Then I shall turn to a cluster of utterances indicating proximity linked to the metaphor of "getting under the skin".

## "Good contact"

Evaluations of how good the contact is with the different patients are being made all the time in the wards, at treatment conferences, at report sessions assessing the patients' day, and in informal conversations between staff members. Here staff may, for instance, tell one another that they do usually have good contact with this patient, who at the moment is aggressive, or on the contrary, they may sigh for the poor or lack of contact that they have managed to achieve with a given patient.

One member of staff expressed the importance of good contact in the following way:

"You cannot get a relationship with the patient if you do not have this good contact sometimes. A lot of what we do here is to create the right relationships. If you never get good contact, in which you sense that you get inside the other, then, I would say, then it is extremely difficult to get on with the treatment process... The more often you have that contact which is open and in which you sense that the patient is letting you into this universe of his that is so strange to you – the more often you are let in there – the easier it becomes to understand what is going on, and the better care you can provide."

"Good contact" was a term that I noted being used very often in the everyday life of the wards. Yet staff had difficulties in defining for me what it actually was. The reason for this, staff explained to me in interviews, was that "good contact" was primarily a feeling. It involved mutual understanding and respect, despite the differences in opinion that they might have. "Good contact" meant having a relationship and knowing each other as individuals.

Staff explained to me the meaning of "good contact" by saying that it was what made it possible to stop patients from flipping out. They also stressed that contact was necessary for the task of judging how dangerous a patient was. It was necessary to have contact before they dared to send a patient to a ward with fewer restrictions. "Good contact" was to be used to get the patient to move on in the treatment process.

Everyone connected contact with results. Without contact, they claimed, it was impossible to reach any result. During the interviews some became less categorical, admitting that with some patients they did in fact send them to open wards or discharged them, despite the fact that they had had poor contact, if any, with them. However, typically in such cases, they said, patients were readmitted later.

When staff were asked to describe situations in which they had had good contact with a patient, they described situations of what Wikan calls "resonance". Resonance is what fosters empathy or compassion, and it requires the application of feelings as well as thoughts. It requires, in Wikan's words, a willingness "to engage with another world, life or idea: an ability to use one's experience [...] to try to grasp or convey meanings that reside neither in words, nor in 'facts', nor text but are evoked in the meeting of one experiencing subject with another..." (1992: 463). Resonance, Wikan says, evokes shared human experience, what people across place and time may have in common. It evokes sameness and a feeling that the intentions of others are heard and responded to, despite differences between the persons in the interplay (ibid. 476). If we add social position and power to place and time as elements that are overcome when there is resonance, then I suggest that resonance corresponds to good contact as staff experienced it.

Another concept to describe the approach that staff in this hospital work with is intersubjectivity. I shall not enter into a large discussion here of intersubjectivity and its roots in phenomenology, but simply point out some elements of the concept and stress the fact that an intersubjective approach lies behind the teaching that staff have undergone. According to Prus (1996: 2), "Intersubjectivity is integral to the human condition. All interpersonal relations, organizational practises [...] are rooted in the human accomplishment of inter-subjectivity". The intersubjective approach rests on the idea that we all have a quest for it. Hence, it becomes an integral part of the nursing, even its very foundation (Dahlberg 1996).

To summarize, the way staff talk about good contact can be seen as an example of how an ideal of nursing as an intersubjective enterprise seeps into practice. Good contact is an ambiguous term referring to intersubjectivity and an interpersonal quest, but in practice staff quickly combine it with other professional tasks, such as preventing aggressive outbursts from patients or obtaining the knowledge they need. As such the term entails the ambiguity inherent in the idea of working towards proximity: it is an aspiration as well as a tool.

Until now, proximity has been seen mostly as a concept linked to intersubjectivity and the ideological roots of psychiatric nursing. Good contact as a concept has been used to refer to what staff and patients have in common, despite their differences, that is, to mutuality and a kind of sameness. Let me now turn to a number of other expressions of proximity and use them to show how this approach is challenged by a simultaneous view of patients as basically role players with a different agenda from that of the staff, and of staff as those who must penetrate behind the mask that patients put on.

## Getting under the skin

The metaphor of "getting under the skin" is often used by staff in the wards. Following Lakoff and Johnson, it can be analysed as a metaphor that reflects and forms the way we perceive the world. In this perspective, "Getting under the skin" becomes a container metaphor grounded in physical and cultural experience (1980: 29). According to Lakoff and Johnson, we are "bounded and set off from the rest of the world by the surface of our skins, and we experience the rest of the world as outside us. Each of us is a container with a bounding surface and an in-out orientation" (ibid.: 29).

The use of the in-out metaphor is very prevalent in Danish society, where thinking of a human being as having an inside and an outside reaches way beyond the physical and far into the psychological and social spheres (see, for instance, Mik-Meyer & Järvinen 2003). The metaphorical essence of the discourse in the wards is just another example of this.

Nursing staff talk about "getting behind the mask" of the patient, about finding out "what is inside the patient" and what "the patient contains". Metaphorically, they thus talk about getting near as "getting inside". "Getting inside" a person is one way to understand proximity. What I find interesting is how this is interlinked metaphorically with "masks" and hence to human beings as role players.

Perhaps it is because they view the patient as having a true essence and a surface that the staff treat intersubjectivity and role play as partly opposing, partly interlinked. This brings confusion to the work because on the one hand staff see their working with and towards proximity as strategic, as part of their role play, but on the other hand they think they only really achieve the knowledge they want when they abandon the role play.

No staff member ever described this schism explicitly as such, though in interviews and lengthy conversations they told me that their task was to play a certain role and at the same time they would problematise the fact that they had patients who had been in the psychiatric system for so long that they had become too skilled in playing their roles. The idea of the mask and the true essence underneath also emerged in the daily discussions of whether patients were trying to cheat (or really were that ill or that healthy) and in staff's descriptions of themselves as being able to see through the patients when the latter tried to hide what was going on inside them. Their descriptions of the role play correspond well to Goffman's description from *Asylums* (1961), of patients who struggle hard to keep back the stage part of their self, while the institution breaks that integrity by creating an environment where everything is put on the front stage (Goffman 1961: 24). The concern with self-representation and the strategic role-player that Goffman has described in his works are issues that staff struggle with (Goffman 1961, 1973).

According to Goffman, patients may evolve what he calls "secondary adjustment", that is, practices that "do not directly challenge staff but allow patients to obtain legal satisfactions by forbidden means or illegal satisfaction by legal means" (1961: 54). Goffman perceives the play of secondary adjustment as providing for the patient "a kind of lodgement of the self" or a means of finding "evidence that he is still his own man, with some control over his environment" (1961: 55). This perception also demonstrates a view of patients as strategic actors with different agendas, as well as of patients who cheat, hide and protect their selves from both the staff and the institution. Inherent in this approach is an "us-them" differentiation. Differences in opinions, aspirations and goals linked to the difference in social status become essential.

Goffman's approach fits well with the staff's descriptions of the interplay as role play, of patients who cheat, hide their selves etc. The staff's problem is that, unlike Goffman, they expect and seek an inner core behind all this, which is only reachable when they get beyond the aspect of play.

Let me now return to the cases of Jakob and Ali in order to illustrate how the above concepts and ideas are played out, negotiated and given meaning in psychiatric praxis. Goffman's concepts of "secondary adjustment", "front" and "contaminative exposure", as well as his description of the involvement circle, will guide us through the analysis.

## Role play and secondary adjustment

Ali had been in the psychiatric system for a good number of years when I met him. He knew the system and its different sub-specialities well as he had become a psychiatric football always being moved between the locked wards of the hospital. He became a forensic patient while hospitalised as he conducted a robbery in a shop nearby. In the forensic wards a pattern of poor contact, and what staff described as confidence on a formal level only, was repeated from earlier stays in ordinary psychiatry. Ali smoked hash and consumed other illegal drugs when he got hold of them. He often escaped, either to take illegal drugs or because staff did not give him the leave he had asked for – for instance, in order to participate in family celebrations. Staff often felt that he abused them and their trust in him, when they showed him any.

Ali had many conflicts with staff and other patients, verbally as well as physically. In some conflicts he would appear angry but normal, while in others he would talk loudly and at length about his special abilities and contact with the gods (who then included Allah, Jesus and gods from Greek mythology).

Ali was one of those who knew well what he was supposed to say – he and the staff agreed on that. He knew what he had to say in order to get more sedatives, in order to obtain access to the garden, and so on. (After all, this was why he was repeatedly able to obtain permission to go for a walk with staff and again and again use this as a chance to escape). Ali could also tell me how important it was to have a good relationship with the staff and would use the same words to describe it as the staff would ("trust, confidence, containing, cooperation"). However, once, when I later asked him how he felt with staff, he exclaimed in a totally different voice, "They can shove it!"

Ali practised secondary adjustment. He played the role of the confident and cooperative patient, but only partly, and always with otherwise unattainable goals as the motivating factor. He had learnt the language of help and staff-patient relations, but when he was asked directly, he said they could "shove" it. The staff, for their part, were experiencing a patient who was playing a false role for them. The problem for Ali was that his secondary adjustment was too explicit. The staff primarily saw a patient who was a nuisance, who cheated them, and in whom they saw no progress.

## Masks and fronts

With Jacob things were different. He is an example of a patient who did not practise secondary adjustment at the beginning of his hospital stay, but rather tried to break the code for the specific relationship he was supposed to have with the staff. In the beginning he chose what Goffman calls "assimilation" as a line of adjustment (1961). This line, however, fitted badly with the perception of patients as having masks and fronts, with which it was confronted.

I met Jakob on his first day in a psychiatric hospital. From the beginning he was very conscious of the power that the staff had over his life. As he explained, the staff regulated his contact with the outside world, so it was important to stay on good terms with them. In the beginning the staff described Jakob as friendly, polite and easy to talk with.

Jakob preferred not to talk about his illness with the staff. To him, this was like crossing a border that kept them at a distance from him, which he wished to do. As the staff were in the ward for eight, sometimes sixteen hours at a stretch, it meant that he would have to be with them after a sensible conversation too. Jakob felt it was better only to break this boundary with people who were involved but who then left the ward again – like the psychiatrist. Jakob had difficulties in getting up in the morning, but otherwise he behaved in an exemplary fashion. He had almost no conflicts with staff or other patients, participated in activities, and took the medicine the doctor prescribed him. After some months, when he had received his sentence, he was to be moved to a less secure ward. For a while the staff discussed among themselves whether they should move Jakob directly to an open ward. Many of them thought that his behaviour suited an open ward. They highlighted the good contact they had with him and their ability to talk with him about everything, including his criminality. But others disagreed, arguing that Jakob had committed a crime so serious that it was far too soon for him to be sent to an open ward after only a couple of months being in a locked one. They also said that Jakob had not shown very much (of his illness or psychotic symptoms), and that it was difficult to know what he "contained". One could not know what he was hiding behind the politeness and friendliness.

As this case shows, patients must "show something", and staff need to know what they "contain". They need to know something that they imagine is there behind the façade before they dare send a patient to an open ward. In the end Jakob was moved to a less secure but still locked ward. The reason for this was not only the above disagreement, it also had to do with the by now growing pressure for beds in open wards. But the idea of "knowing" the patient – or in this case not knowing him – became a powerful argument that cancelled out his friendliness, cooperative attitude and the good contact that some of the staff had experienced with him.

It is also worth paying attention to Jakob's own interpretation of his situation. Jakob understood how powerful his relationship with the staff was, and he thought he knew what was expected by him – a relationship that was friendly and comfortable; he tried to adjust to that. However, over time he learnt what was at stake, and that this relationship demanded something else from him. He became still more aware of the role play that goes on between patients and staff, and how "knowing" is a part of this.

## Contaminative exposure

Jakob's attention to the role play was followed by a change in his line of adjustment. From assimilation he changed to the intransigent line, until he found a way to conduct a form of secondary adjustment similar to the one the other patients used, including Ali. According to Goffman, patients usually use a combination of different lines of adjustment in order to have the highest possible chance of getting through the system mentally and physically unharmed (1961: 64f). In this perspective, patients appear as strategically motivated, choosing how to enter situations. For Jakob, however, the shifts did not seem to be strategic, but were rather reactions to situations that affected him mentally.

In the beginning of his stay, Jakob said that he often decided to overlook it when he felt unjustly treated, because such little things meant so little in the larger perspective. He clearly believed that he understood the relationship, his situation and what it demanded. However, this changed as he moved to a new ward.

Jakob got off on the wrong foot in his new ward. When he had been there for a month, I came to visit him. As the very first thing, he exclaimed: "Look around – this is a rubbish ward!" Then he continued by saying how restrictive the ward was. It was that bad, when he saw staff now he identified them with all the restrictions, and that made it impossible for him to relate to them as individuals or enter into a confident relationship with them. Jakob said that he knew he was the one who was blocking the development of a relationship. When staff sat down beside him and asked him how things had been in the patient workshop, he just answered, "Fine". And when they asked him what he had been doing, he just answered, "Nothing special". "I know, I end the conversation that way", Jakob told me," but I just do not want to talk with them!" I reminded Jakob that earlier he had grumbled about patients who could not abstract from the rules. That seemed forgotten now. Jakob continued by telling me about humiliating body searches and the noisy silence of his walks with members of staff.

Jakob's descriptions seem to be in accordance with what Goffman called "contaminative exposure", which describes how patients feel exposed and invaded by certain practices in the ward, including having to be in view at all times, and being forced into social relationships and activities which have symbolic implications that are incompatible with the patients' sense of self (1961:28). According to Goffman, contaminative exposure is a central reason for patients' need to preserve a lodgement for the self outside the clutches of the institution, and hence for their tendency to conduct secondary adjustment. In this perspective, Jakob's shift in his adjustment line from the friendly patient to the impolite and irreconcilable patient seems to be a reaction to his experience of invasion. As we shall see later, Jakob learnt over time to preserve a lodgement for the self much like Ali did.

## The involvement circle

Soon, Jakob learnt two new aspects of his special relationship with the staff: the balance between distance and proximity, and the meaning of "knowing".

In *Asylums*, Goffman writes ironically that there is always a certain risk that an inmate will appear human (1961: 81). Sometimes staff experience the patient as someone they like, but he may then violate the moral world of the staff even more by his behaviour and his illness because the violation seems much greater when it is committed by someone who is a part of one's own moral world. Hence, warmth and attachment is often followed by distance from the patient, and in this way, Goffman states, a circle of repeated alternation between distance and proximity is created.

When Goffman studied psychiatry back in the 1950s, staff were supposed to keep their distance from the patients. Closeness was seen as a "mistake", though a natural one in working with human beings (ibid.). In contemporary psychiatry closeness is a goal, and the contradictory alternation between distance and proximity has become part of the professional approach. Staff must learn to balance professional distance and close empathy in order to be there for the patient without invading him, while maintaining the capacity to see things from outside and act upon it. Proximity is important in psychiatric care, but there is also a danger of being overwhelmed by psychotic people's frustrations and difficult life circumstances. Hence a certain distance is needed, according to the main theoretician of this approach (Strand 1994: 83-6). From a more practical point of view, Handy observes that nursing staff in contemporary psychiatry are expected to use themselves and enter into a close and demanding relationship, but also that they regularly evade the task by engaging in administrative work when the relationship becomes too demanding (Handy 1991). The involvement circle can thus be found in contemporary psychiatry, though in a reversed form.

## Distance and proximity in practice

According to Strand (1994), the balance between distance and proximity is one that staff must create. It is also one that patients must discover and come to accept. When patients do not find an appropriate balance, they are described by staff as "staff-seeking" or as "isolating themselves". They are criticised for misunderstanding the relationship when they call their contact person among the staff their "sister", but also when they see the staff as guards (Jacobsen & Johansen 2002). Since staff often take the balance as given but seldom tell patients about it, it is often difficult for the latter to find and accept the balance. Jakob's story exemplifies this.

Staff in the new ward perceived Jakob quite differently from the staff in the old ward. At conferences they described a man who was only façade, who hid himself behind an impeccable surface, but who was not like that at all in reality, a man whom they absolutely did not want to let out of the ward. As one member of staff said to the doctor, "This neat man with the neat clothes is not neat at all when confronted with his crime".

It emerged that, to a large extent, the conflict Jakob had with the staff in the new ward was one between himself and his contact person among the staff, a conflict over the boundaries of proximity and distance. I accordingly decided to follow the case up through interviews with both the contact person and Jakob himself.

When Jakob came to the ward, the staff member who was to become his contact person read through his criminal and medical records. The contact person formed the impression that, even though Jakob had committed his crime while he had been very ill, he had to relate to it at some time, and he could see from the medical record that this had not happened yet. So one day he decided that the time had come to confront Jakob with his crime.

The contact person was taken by surprise by Jakob's reaction. Jakob gave details for a full hour about what had happened, what he was thinking at the time and about his scruples. The contact person had to stop the conversation because of other duties he had in the ward. Two hours later, Jakob went to the contact person and scolded him. The contact person felt that Jakob was trying to demean him by scolding him for doing the job of a psychologist without having the necessary education. Afterwards the contact person wondered why Jakob had not simply stood back, but had told everything. "We all stand back with something when we narrate", he explained to me, "he could have done that".

Jakob had crossed his own boundary of distance from the staff and that of the staff member as well. Certainly he should talk, but not so much and not in that way. His story illustrates well, I suggest, how painful an experience it may be to find the right balance between proximity and distance in this field.

Jakob was not the only patient who experienced a demand for knowledge that he did not wish to give and that he did not know the proportions of. Many patients described to me encountering a demand from staff that they "open up", and they could entertain me with stories about how long it had taken them to accept this. One patient claimed it had taken him two years. Hence, the learning process that I followed with Jakob seems to be a concern of patients in general, who in different ways strive to learn what kind of "openness" is expected from them and what is needed to make progress in the system.

At the same time, patients are very much aware that staff should not come to know too much about them. There is a fear that if the staff find out too much, if they become too close, they might observe something that might lead to the patient being kept hospitalised. Ali described this well in a conversation on the differences between ethnic Danish and ethnic foreign patients. He said:

"What is in here (placing his hand on his breast) you will never get a Muslim to talk about, and not a Dane either. It is so for everyone, you just don't do it, because if you do, it will turn back on you badly. It is a matter of protecting oneself ... I have let a lot out from here (the heart), and I have been punished for it". The punishment, Ali explained, consisted of prolonged hospitalisation. "The smart ones are those who keep to themselves, and just take a little bit of medicine. They are soon discharged. They are the smart ones!"

"Muslims don't open so much up. They don't tell everybody about sex, for example, as the Danes do...." Ali blushed and excused himself. "It was just an example", he said. I helped him continue by asking if there were other topics that Muslims did not talk about. "Yes", he answered, family problems and personal problems, though I do because I am integrated; I tell everything because everyone should be able to follow me". Then Ali told me a long and confusing tale about how he was a special person with special abilities, and that was the reason why everybody must be able to follow him. He soon talked himself into a narrative about his contacts to all the gods that he often repeated.

Ali had a hard struggle determining how much he should tell staff. The manner in which he fell into his own psychotic universe when talking about it shows in its own way how painful it was for him to find the right balance. Jakob also struggled to find out how much or how well staff needed to know him, and sometimes he seemed to play with the balance.

One day Jakob told me that all his problems in the new ward were connected to the fact that he refused to talk about his criminality with his contact person. Jakob felt that it was of no use to talk about that episode again. He had had to tell it so many times in the court. Now he just needed to put it behind him. But his contact person had told him that he had to talk about it with him again, in order to ensure that he did not commit such an act again. "But", Jakob said, "what do they mean by that? They don't know me at all here, so how can they judge that?"

Jakob might not have understood the play of balancing distance and proximity at that time, but he had a clear idea of what the play – or game – was about: that staff could only make assessments according to how well they knew him. In this way "knowing" became for Jakob, as for the other patients, a part of the play with staff over control, something that one could pretend or hide – or show something of in order to "obtain legal satisfaction by forbidden means or illegal satisfaction by legal means" (Goffman 1961: 54). In other words, knowing was given a central position in the secondary adjustment that patients conducted, so that the patient as a man with a mask and with something behind it was created and re-created as a living cultural construct.

## Conclusions

Jakob's and Ali's stories show how patients may become caught up in staff's view of them as role-players with masks behind which they hide their essences, but also how patients themselves, for reasons associated with their experiences of being locked up and controlled, enter into a form of play that supports that perception. The play is basically about control and knowing, and is based on the idea that patients possess some inner core that can be shown and known, but also hidden.

Their stories also make it clear that not only staff but also patients work to balance proximity and distance; thus working towards proximity is characterised by mutual strategic and conscious interaction. The two cases seem to show a fundamental difference in staff-patient positions and a strategic interaction based on it rather than a quest for mutual understanding on the grounds of what all human beings have in common, as the ideological, intersubjective approach to nursing would have it.

As this article has demonstrated, psychiatric nursing staff seem to be caught in a paradox, as on the one hand they understand proximity as a kind of intersubjectivity that is "true" and are driven by a quest for it, but on the other hand see this intersubjectivity as opposed to and challenged by the strategic role-playing that patients are believed to resort to all too often, yet which staff themselves like to explain as something that they play as part of their job.

As in paradoxes of the kind that Bateson describes (1973), the problem is that in interaction (or communication), they simultaneously refer to two different meta contexts, each of which opposes the other. Proximity refers to an intersubjective quest and universal human understanding, despite differences in time, place and social position. At the meta level, it communicates the idea that difference is dissolved between us and them, in the present case, between patients and staff in the psychiatric wards. As Wikan says, it evokes sameness. At the same time, however, the right balance of proximity is a tool for staff to acquire knowledge, as well as for patients to move towards discharge. In other words, it is a requisite, a tool in a role play. At the meta level, the role play evokes difference. The difference between us and them is at the core of the whole process: it is negotiated, played with, defined and redefined, but not dissolved. At the first level, trust, honesty and truth are communicated. At the second level are cheating, hiding, strategies and secondary adjustment. So in concrete interaction, how is one to interpret what? How is one to know when one has "really" come near a patient? And as a patient, how is one to be trusted? By pointing out this paradox, I do not intend to criticise nursing staff for having an ambivalent attitude to their patients. What I wish to point out is that the existing theories of proximity and distance as nursing staff have been taught them leave out important aspects when they deal with these phenomena as existential in nature while overlooking the cultural and social dynamics that inform – and sometimes destroy – the process of working towards proximity.

## References

Andersen, K.V.

2003 Invandrerbørn leger dårligt: Institutionel konstruktion af farlig fritid. In: N. Mik-Meyer & M. Järvinen (eds.) *At skabe en klient*. Copenhagen: Hans Reitzels Forlag, pp. 136-161.

Anderson, S.

2000 *I en klasse for sig*. Copenhagen: Hans Reitzels Forlag.

Bateson, G.

1973 *Steps to an ecology of mind*. St. Albans: Paladin.

Dahlberg, K.

1996 Intersubjective meeting in holistic caring: A Swedish perspective. *Nursing Science Quarterly* 9, 4: 147-151.

Foucault, M.

1995 [1975] *Discipline and punish: The birth of the prison*. New York: Vintage Books.

Goffman, E.

1961 *Asylums. Essays on the social situation of mental patients and other inmates*. New York: Anchor Books, Doubleday.

1973 *Presentation of self in everyday life*. Woodstock, New York: Overlook.

Handy, J.

1991 The social context of occupational stress in a caring profession. *Social Science and Medicine* 32, 2: 819-830.

Hummelvold, J.K

1982 *Helt – ikke stykvist og delt*. Oslo: Gyldendal.

Jacobsen, C. & Johansen, K.

2002 *Kulturmøde i psykiatrien*. Roskilde, Denmark: Sct. Hans Hospital.

Lakoff, G. & Johnson, M.

1980 *Metaphors we live by*. Chicago: The University of Chicago Press.

Martinsen, K.

2003 *Fenomenologi og omsorg: Tre dialoger*. Oslo: Universitetsforlaget.

Mik-Meyer, N.

2003 Anne er sygdomsfikseret. In: N. Mik-Meyer & M. Järvinen (eds.) *At skabe en klient*. Copenhagen: Hans Reitzels Forlag, pp. 82-107.

Mik-Meyer, N. & Järvinen, M.

2003 *At skabe en klient: Institutionelle identiteter i socialt arbejde*. Copenhagen: Hans Reitzels Forlag.

Poulsen, H.D., Gottlieb, P. & Adserballe, H.

2000 *Ret og tvang i psykiatrien*. Copenhagen: Munksgaard.

Prus, R.

1996 *Symbolic interaction and ethnographic research: Intersubjectivity and the study of human lived experience*. New York: State University of New York Press.

Strand, L.

1994 *Fra kaos mod mestring, samling og helhed: psykiatrisk sygepleje til psykotiske patienter*. Copenhagen: Gyldendal.

Wikan, U.

1992 Beyond the words: The power of resonance. *American Ethnologist* 19, 3: 460-482.

## Parents' first encounter with their preemie: Distance or devotion?

Jónína Einarsdóttir

### Introduction

The popular maternal bonding theory holds that mother love originates in childbirth. According to the theory, the first minutes and hours of life are a "sensitive period" for establishment of maternal affection because of the post-partum hormonal status of mothers (Klaus et al. 1972, Klaus et al. 1995, Klaus & Kennell 1976). Maternal bonding theory assumes that if the mother is allowed to be close to her infant directly after birth she takes advantage of a "whole system" with which she is equipped and allows her "to communicate with her infant in ways that can bypass the logical and rational areas of the brain and allow [her] to take in and sense the baby at a deeper, more primitive level" (Klaus et al. 1995: 86). On the other hand, without explaining any further details, fathers are said to become "attached to their new infants in their own ways" (ibid.: 74)[16].

Maternal bonding theory attributes disorder in child development, in addition to child abuse and neglect, to inadequate maternal bonding, and it has been used to advocate changes in routines in maternity wards and child care institutions (Eyer 1992, Crouch & Manderson 1995). However, empirically, maternal bonding theory has been difficult to verify and studies have come to contradictory results. Research has failed to demonstrate that children who did not have an early contact with their mothers immediately after birth are in higher risk of neglect or abuse than those who did (Field 1996). Recent review of studies on the importance of early skin-to-skin contact for mothers and infants highlights lack in methodological quality, disparities in the implementation of the contact, and variation in outcome (Anderson et al. 2003). So-called attachment outcomes showed little or no difference between mothers who had an early skin-to-skin contact with their infants and those who did not. Yet early skin-to-skin contact appears to prolong breastfeeding and decrease infant crying significantly.

Maternal bonding theory presupposes that human females respond to their infants in the same way as female sheep and goats, and reject their offspring

---

[16] See Mackey & Immerman (2004) and Roggman (2004) for discussion on biological foundations for father-child relationship as different from mother-child relationship.

if separated from them immediately postpartum. Klopfer (1996) demonstrates the danger in extrapolating assumptions about human maternal behaviour from the behaviours of other animals, as there are variations even within under-groups of the same species. He points out that even within *Homo sapiens* maternal behaviour may be highly context related. The sociobiologist Hrdy (1999) argues that "bonding" in terms of biologically based affection established during a "sensitive period" after birth is unlikely to evolve in humans or even other primates. She maintains that in humans, "unlike sheep, bonding right after birth is by no means essential for the development of love. It can, however, facilitate the process" (ibid.: 488). Nonetheless, Hrdy states that "a mother's commitment to her infant – and in the case of humans, this is what we mean by 'mother love' – is neither a myth nor a cultural construct" (ibid.: 315). She argues, "mothers evolved not to produce as many children as they could but to trade off quantity for quality, or to achieve a secure status, and in that way increase the chance that at least a few offspring will survive and prosper" (ibid.: 10). Hrdy emphasizes innate maternal responses to infant cues and stresses the importance of innate maternal responses to infant appearances:

"Certain kinds of cries, given by premature infants seem to be universally disturbing, even aversive, while rounded heads and plumb features are universally appealing. The sight of a defective newborn is profoundly disturbing. Even low-birth weight babies are distressing and generate psychological distress." (ibid.: 457)

Hrdy recognizes however certain exceptions that "innate responses" cannot explain, such as "the many modern mothers" who constrained by the tenets of so-called ethical behaviour act against nature and self-interest and "throw themselves utterly and wholeheartedly into care of babies unlikely to survive" (ibid.: 459f.). Other mothers, "natural" and unconcerned about ethics, appear to act in response to innate impulses in line with their evolved nature (ibid.: 56f., 114, 376ff.).

In contrast to Hrdy, Scheper-Hughes argues that "mother love is anything other than natural and instead represents a matrix of images, meanings, sentiments, and practices that are everywhere socially and culturally produced" (Scheper-Hughes 1992: 341). She maintains that emotions are only comprehensible within the framework of culture[17], and rejects all theories that assume the "naturalness" of mother-infant relations, inclusive "the hegemonic

[17] See Lutz & Abu-Lughod (1990), Abu-Lughod (1993), and Lutz (1988).

biomedical model of maternal bonding" (ibid.: 412). Scheper-Hughes argues that Brazilian shanty town mothers selectively neglect their weakest and less attractive children to death, thus allocating scarce resources for the survival of stronger ones. This occurs through delayed and gradual attachment and "suspension of the ethical." Scheper-Hughes expects "to discover some resonances and resemblances with mothering practices at other times and places" (ibid.: 342). She argues that her findings challenge theories "proposing essential, or universal, womanly scripts" such as the maternal bonding theory and feminist theories that advocate women's virtues (1992: 401). Scheper-Hughes maintains that mother love "as we know and understand it" is an invention related to "the rise of the modern, bourgeois, nuclear family ... but also ... with the precipitous decline in infant mortality and female fertility" (ibid.: 401). According to Scheper-Hughes "modern notions of mother love derive in the first instance from a 'new' reproductive 'strategy': to give birth to few infants and to 'invest' heavily (emotionally as well as materially) in each one from birth onward" (ibid.: 401f.). In the opposite, where child mortality and fertility are high, the reproductive strategy is to have many children but "to invest selectively in those considered the 'best bets' for survival in terms of preferred sex, birth order, appearance, health or perceived viability" (ibid.: 402). This, Scheper-Hughes argues, requires cultural construction of maternal thinking that allows fatal neglect of weak infants and thus spares mothers the grief following "the death of each and every fragile child" (ibid.: 402), and she concludes: "I have no doubt ... that the local culture is organized to defend women against the psychological ravaging of grief, I assume that the culture is quite successful in doing so" (ibid.: 430).

Scheper-Hughes affirms that the process of delayed maternal attachment applies only to poor women; for the better-off middle class women in her study area "child death is as shocking and aberrant as for affluent women anywhere else in the world" (ibid.: 328). In contrast, for Hrdy (1999) selective neglect and outright infanticide are adaptive reproductive strategies not only for the poor but also for the economically better off. In her arguing there is a notion of the "noble savage" mother who allows innate impulses to drive her to neglect or dispose her "low-quality" infants, in opposition to the modern Western mother.

Elsewhere I have discussed the relevance of Scheper-Hughes' and Hrdy's arguing for maternal reactions to child death in Biombo region, Guinea-Bissau, where every third child is likely to die before the age of five (Einarsdóttir 2004). In this chapter I present the experiences of "modern" parents' (to use Hrdy's classification mentioned above) first encounter with their extremely low birth-weight infants (1000 grams or less) in Iceland. This chapter is based on a fieldwork conducted in a neonatal intensive care unit (NICU)[18]. Homes, day-care centres and treatment facilities of infants born 1000 grams or less were visited and qualitative interviews taken with professionals (physicians, nurses, assistant nurses, physiotherapists, pre-school teachers, 28 mothers and 25 fathers (of 35 children (29 births) born from September 1, 1998 to August 31, 2002), and other family members. I begin this chapter with descriptions of parents' first encounter with their preterm tiny infant. Then I discuss their reaction to that encounter and theories concerned with maternal reactions to unviable births.

## Face-to-face

Most, but not all, of the parents with whom I discussed the first encounter with their preemie vividly remember when they entered NICU to see their newborn infant for the first time. Frequently the mother and the father went together for that occasion. Yet, several fathers were the first to see the infant as the mothers were unable to go to the unit after having had a caesarean operation. One of the mothers died after birth, which is an extremely rare event in Iceland. Several mothers were admitted to an intensive care unit themselves as their life was in danger, which put the fathers in a very stressful situation. Some of the fathers spent the first days after birth running between the intensive care units for neonates and adults in an attempt to follow the condition of both the mother and infant. They also had the responsibility to keep other family members informed about the situation and latest news.

A few fathers admitted that considering the information given before birth they had almost taken for given that their infant would die, thus they were far more concerned about the condition of their wife than that of the premie. A father whose wife was in intensive care for three days said: "I have so much to be grateful for, and still today I call him my little bonus. I did not expect him to be born. He came. I did not expect him to survive … or I only thought about his mother … but I got him as a bonus."

---

[18] The Research Council of Iceland (Rannis) funded the research on which this article is based. Centre for Child Health Services in Reykjavík and Institute of Anthropology, University of Iceland, were guest institutions for the research project. The Icelandic Data Protection Authority and the Ethic Committee of National University Hospital in Reykjavik granted requested ethical permissions. Parents and professionals who participated in the study are all gratefully acknowledged.

Fathers, who went alone to see the infant after birth, told the mother about the baby. Their description varied in details and at times they admitted to have consciously reported better news than they felt justified so as not to make her too worried. Indeed, some of the mothers were aware of this: "He said everything was fine, and that our children were beautiful, but he was not convincing. He looked tired and distressed," a mother of twins explained. Another mother, who also got the news that "everything was fine," was relieved. She noticed that her husband came back genuinely happy and told her that the baby was such a beautiful girl. Likewise the routine of staff to always give congratulations with a newborn, independent of the child's situation, was mainly interpreted as an optimistic sign, though at times perceived as odd considering the seriousness of the situation.

"What a tiny baby" may have been the most common statement about the appearance of the infant, followed with comments about all the tools and technical apparatus to which the baby was attached. A father said: "She was extremely small, yes … like a pack of half a kilogram of margarine." Another father said: "She was connected to all these tools. That caused me to feel so bad. I knew she was small, like a pack of margarine. What a miracle that she was alive. We asked for urgent baptism. We wanted at least to give the child a name." Still another father did not mention anything about his infant's appearance but admitted he had asked God to help him keep his baby. There were more parents who admitted to have put their faith in God at this moment.

Even though the infant's tiny body and the technical apparatus were frequently mentioned by parents, many commented on the infant's physical appearance. Both mothers and fathers emphasized that their infant was beautiful and surely was their son or daughter. A young father explained how he gazed into the incubator. "Then I saw the most beautiful child I have ever seen," he said. Contradictory statements are sometimes found. A father said his twin-daughters were really "cute" but at the same time he found them to be "a foetus-like" and in fact "not so beautiful." The mother of the same twin-sisters said they were "healthy-looking" and added as an explanation that it might have been the "parental nature" that made her think like that. Another mother said: "she [my child] was much more beautiful than I expected. I have seen smaller babies and she did not have these outstanding eyes and the particular preemie-look."

Few parents, who thought their infant was somewhat alien and not so human-like, said the infant was more like a bird, chicken, ET or a fetus. A young father, who sat for hours looking at his child in the incubator said: "I noticed at once that he was bigger than the other infants and I felt that was positive. I found him to be a child. Was he my child? Yes, but it was difficult with this glass in between. He had a kind of alien look. It came to my mind."

Several parents made a comment on the completeness of the infant's body. A mother was surprised to see that her son had a lot of hair "after such a short gestation." Some parents took a good time just controlling details – counting toes and fingers. A mother described: "My baby was so tiny and almost transparent. I looked at the fingers and ears and everything. The only thing I could do was to look and hope."

There are, however, mothers who best remember the pain, nausea, tiredness and fatigue when sitting face-to-face with their infant for the first time. The chair was uncomfortable. The heat and noise was threatening. A mother who had been admitted at the intensive care unit also felt ashamed:

"I was feeling such a pain and I did not want to tell anybody about it. I had no energy and felt indifferent. I felt so much pain when trying to see my children and I only wanted to go back to my bed. The incubator was too high and I wanted to come closer to see them. Every movement was so painful and difficult."

Nurses, preoccupied with the fact that mothers do not have an immediate contact postpartum, tend to use this first face-to-face encounter to evaluate mother's ability to bond. Seeing an indifferent and worn-out mother is interpreted as a bad sign for bonding.

Indeed, there were few mothers who were thinking about the possibility of not bonding. A young mother became interned at the intensive care for three days after having passed weeks of pain before giving birth. She described to me all the details when she entered the neonatal intensive unit. She commented on the arrangement of furniture, named all the infants admitted and mentioned she had seen a mother breastfeeding her infant. Then, she looked at her own newborn, which is her second child:

"I did not consider him to be a child … and not my child. I was not a real mother and I felt ashamed because I did not love him. Now it is different. Now he has been at home and I have been with him so much and all that. I could not stay for more than five minutes with him. I was completely exhausted in a wheelchair and the seats were bad and the high pitched sound and everything made me feel bad. I had not done anything for that child and it would have lived even though I would have died."

This mother did not want to touch her child: "… this tiny foot and leg were nothing. Would I touch him and my fingers were coarse. One physical contact does not change anything. Bonding begins at home," she said. This mother, who knew the maternal bonding theory through her professional life, rejected the importance of immediate bonding in favour of gradual attachment.

A couple of mothers who also knew about the bonding theory were somewhat worried about the possibility that they might not bond due to lack of contact with the infant postpartum. Still, they were confident that after all lack of postpartum contact did not negatively affect their maternal affection. A few mothers admitted, when confronted with the theory, that they had little faith in such a science. After I had explained the theory to a mother who had never heard about it before, she commented: "What rubbish." How could an event such as premature birth reduce her affection for her child, she wondered? It would rather be the opposite, she argued, an opinion stated by more parents.

Not all parents wanted to touch their infant during the first visit and they tended to feel bad about it. Young father explained: "I did not want to touch him. I don't know why. He was a kind of fragile lying there like a stillborn and this was of course only shock to me. At once after leaving the room I felt terribly ashamed not having touched him." Parents who did not want to touch their infant at the first visit explained their reluctance with fear to hurt the infant or to cause it infection. Thinness of the skin was also mentioned as a reason for their reluctance to touch the infant.

Most parents accepted however to touch their infant. A father of two was relieved to see his daughter. She was "tiny" but otherwise she looked very much like his other children when they were newborn, he said, and he did not hesitate and stroke her foot, as did many, when he was offered to do so. Young mother maintained that her baby had reacted to her presence. She was one of those exhausted mothers from the intensive care unit. She remembered all the physical pain but also her eagerness to see her newborn infant. She explained: "I was finally allowed to go to see my baby and it was a kind of excitement – not fear. I only remember that I took his hand and he turned his head and smiled and grasped my finger." The infant's grasping of the finger was mentioned by more parents as a sign of hope.

Parents who were shocked to see their infant for the first time, due to the bodily features, pointed out that they were very quick to adapt to the infant's appearance. The second occasion was much easier. Many commented on their own surprise later when other family members showed a strong reaction to the appearance of the infant.

Considering the information given before birth, for many of the parents it was already a victory that their child had survived the first hours after birth. A first-time father said: "I was very pleased to see him and this was my boy. It was just a matter of fighting for survival." While some parents emphasized the positive signs, for instance the infant being "chubby," "bigger than others," or having "a strong will" which was quite a common statement, others thought of their preemie as vulnerable, helpless, as stillborn or almost dead. Parents did not all share the same optimism about the future. A mother, who found her daughter really beautiful "despite all the tools and equipments around" was nonetheless shocked seeing her. "Somebody [referring to the physicians] is cheating on me. This child cannot survive," she said. The information that such a tiny infant had some chance of survival could not be true.

All the parents in the study hoped for survival and cure independent on their conceptions about the physical appearance of the child and independent of circumstances of pregnancy. Most parents expressed their faith in the medical science. Yet, at the same time, many mentioned having prayed to God for help. A few wondered if death could be a better alternative than life.

## Parental reactions – distance or devotion?

Weiss (1998) highlights the importance of appearance for parental acceptance of their infants born in Israeli hospitals. She describes how mothers examine the newborn checking "his/her body limb by limb, make comments on the coloring, size, weight, number, cleanliness, perfection and proportion" (ibid.: 194). Questions such as "Not missing anything?" or "Is that normal?" are asked. Weiss gives also examples about parental commenting on their physically impaired infants as "ugly thing," "monster," and "dead for us". Of 350 children with appearance abnormalities at birth reported by Weiss about 2/3 were abandoned by their parents. When it concerns premature infants, Weiss maintains that the parents' "pulling back from their preemies is related, first of all, to the size of the baby" (ibid.: 203). The apparatus surrounding the baby is also a contributory factor. Weiss maintains that for premature babies, as with physically abnormal babies, the appearance, not the severity of the infant's illness, is the factor that primarily shapes parental attitudes. After a successful cosmetic repair of the defect parents are likely to accept their child. Nonetheless, Weiss rejects both bonding and socio-biology as models for understanding the parental reaction to the appearance of their infants. She suggests that the difference in the child's physical form “is capable of producing a cognitive dissonance powerful enough to disrupt the existing order of things – a disruption so essential as to result in the stigmatization of the appearance-impaired child as a “non-person” and hence lead to his/her rejection” (ibid.: 206). What happens is that deformity is taken to reflect some vital inborn quality.

In line with the above, the parents in my study were very much concerned about the infant’s size. The technical equipment attached to the baby also attracted parental attention and symbolized the threatening situation. However, none of these attributes contributed to the rejection of the infant. Rather the opposite was a fact. Indeed, while some parents stressed the somewhat alien features of the infant’s body many reacted positively to its completeness. Emotionally, many parents became overwhelmed by the vulnerability and helplessness of the infant, something that contributed to feelings of sympathy and affection. While describing the infant, parents almost never used the concept person or personhood. In fact, only one father wondered if his infant, who died, was not a person. However, qualities related to personality were stressed and even seen as more important for survival than physical or bodily appearance. Parents frequently attributed to their infant characteristics such as vitality and strength, qualities that were central in the struggle for life. Without these qualities the infant would not have survived, parents argued.

In addition to the fighting spirit attributed to the infant, parents’ faith in survival was also based on hope, wishful thinking or an alternative knowledge. Dreams, new and old ones, were reinterpreted in the light of new experience. Parents, other family members or friends visited spiritual medium for information about the infant’s future life and alternative, additional, help to that offered at the NICU. In addition, parents engaged in finding an appropriate name for their infant, often a name that indicated strength, love and life. Parents who before birth had decided to brake away from the Icelandic tradition to give their child a grandparent’s name or some important name within the family changed their mind. The name that had already been chosen before birth was also at times given a new meaning. Most parents whose children were in particular danger choose baptism, and it was often interpreted as a turning-point to the better. On the other hand, it was also taken to be a surrender or an acknowledgement of the possibility of death and thus resisted. The reluctance of family members and friends to give birth presents and congratulate parents were with some dismay taken as a lack of faith in life, which contributed to feelings of distance.

Having a miscarriage or giving birth to a stillborn or preterm infant is not something well-informed mothers are prepared for. The anthropologist Layne (2003: 1881) maintains that the "images of beautiful, sensual, pregnant, ultra-womanly women, surrounded by loving partners, friends, children, and birth attendants, giving birth naturally in warm supportive environments, in spiritual harmony and erotic bliss to healthy, ready-to-bond, ready-to-nurse babies" shapes the expectations of mothers. In Iceland images of natural birth in a homelike atmosphere are commonly found in books and brochures on pregnancy and birth. The importance of uniting mother and infant after birth for establishment of mother-infant bonding is stressed. Premature birth does not allow this to happen. There were a few mothers who expressed some preoccupation having not been able to have a close postpartum contact with their infants. However, they argued the theory did at least not conform to their experience.

## Conclusion

In this presentation I have described the immediate reactions of parents when they experience the first face-to-face encounter with their preemie born 1000 grams or less in Iceland. While the word devotion clearly demonstrates the reactions of many parents, who recognise the infant as truly "their child," others express a notion of distance. Indeed, parental reactions were at times ambivalent or contradictory, simultaneously characterised by devotion and distance. Despite the particular physical appearance, the so-called preemie-look that characterizes infants born prematurely mentioned by Hrdy (1999), many parents found their preemie beautiful and most were surprised over the completeness of the infant's body, inclusive those who recognised their infant as somewhat alien. Indeed, thinking of one's infant as a stranger is commonly found among mothers who see their full term infant for the first time.

While many parents did not give much for the bonding theory, the few mothers who had worried about their own lack of bonding due to the circumstances of birth were confident that at least it did not apply to them. For them, being distant to the baby during the "sensitive period" did not erode their maternal dedication. Klaus et al. (1995) argue that fathers become "attached to their new infants in their own ways." I am tempted to consider if one can claim that mothers become attached to their newborn "in their own ways" as well.

**References**

Abu-Lughod, L.

1993 *Writing women's worlds: Bedouin stories.* Berkeley: University of California Press.

Anderson, G. C.; Moore, E.; Hepworth, J. & Bergman, N.

2003 Early skin-to-skin contact for mothers and their healthy newborn infants. *Cochrane Database of Systematic Reviews* 2: CD003519.

Crouch, M. & Manderson, L.

1995 The social life of bonding theory. *Social Science and Medicine* 41, 6: 837-44.

Einarsdóttir, J.

2004 *Tired of weeping. Mother love, child death, and poverty in Guinea-Bissau.* Madison, Wisconsin: University of Wisconsin Press.

Eyer, D. E.

1992 *Mother infant bonding: A scientific fiction.* New Haven, London: Yale University Press.

Field, T.

1996 Attachment and separation in young children. *Annu. Rev. Psychol.* 47: 541-61.

Hrdy, S. B.

1999 *Mother nature: A history of mothers, infants, and natural selection.* New York: Pantheon Books.

Klaus, M.; Jerauld, R.; Kreger, N.; McAlpine, W.; Steffa, M. & Kennell, J.

1972 Maternal attachment: importance of the first postpartum days. *New England Journal of Medicine* 286: 460-3.

Klaus, M. H. & Kennell, J. H. (eds.)

1976 *Maternal-infant bonding*. St. Louis: C.V. Mosby Co.

Klaus, M. H.; Kennell, J. H. & Klaus, P. H.

1995 *Bonding: Building the foundations of secure attachment and independence*. New York: Merloyd Lawrence Book, Addison-Wesley Publishing Company.

Klopfer, P. H.

1996 "Mother Love" revisited: On the use of animal models. *American Scientist* 84, 4: 391-321.

Layne, L. L.

2003 Unhappy endings: a feminist reappraisal of the women's health movement from the vantage of pregnancy loss. *Social Science and Medicine* 56, 9: 1881-91.

Lutz, C. & Abu-Lughod, L. (eds.)

1990 *Language and the politics of emotion*. Cambridge: Cambridge University Press.

Lutz, C. A.

1988 *Unnatural emotions: Everyday sentiments on a Micronesian atoll and their challenge to Western theory*. Chicago: University of Chicago Press.

Mackey, W. C. & Immerman, R. S.

2004 The Foundation of the father-to-child relationship. *Mankind Quarterly* 45, 1: 47.

Roggman, L. A.

2004 Do fathers just want to have fun? *Human Development* 47, 4: 228.

Scheper-Hughes, N.

1992 *Death without weeping: The violence of everyday life in Brazil.* Berkeley: University of California Press.

Weiss, M.

1998 Parents' rejection of their appearance-impaired newborns: Some critical observations regarding the social myth of bonding. *Marriage and Family Review* 27, 3-4: 191-209.

## Feelings, distance and emotions in medical practice[19]

Josep M. Comelles

Translated by Susan M. DiGiacomo

"Ne manipulez jamais en présence d'un profane, pas de religion sans mystères."

(Docteur Munaret 1840: 236)[20]

For years, writers and social scientists have emphasised the feelings of patients. Perhaps we have forgotten about those of physicians. Over the past two decades in Western societies, there has been increasing talk about "burnout" in the health professions, accompanied by increasingly vocal criticism of medical practice. It tends to be a consequence of overcrowded medical facilities, shortage of time, and a consequent reduction in communication between patients, doctors, and patients' relatives. The conflicts generated in these two contexts have filled the recent professional literature with articles on "burnout syndrome"[21]. Criticism of doctors is not a new phenomenon; we can find it in several forms, both written and graphic, from classical Rome to the present. What has changed is the nature of the criticism.

Before the second half of the twentieth century, doctors were better able to accept the limits of their profession:

"The sick-chamber will henceforth be the theatre of your labours, the scene alike of your triumphs and of your failures; for it is there, amidst the groans and the sufferings of your fellow creatures, that you are to reign, and to ac-

---

[19] I wish to thank Susan DiGiacomo for her excellent work as a translator but especially for her extraordinary critical skills as an editor – in the English sense of the word – for which no thanks are ever sufficient. I have been able to incorporate only in part her comments and comparative perspective based on American sources because many of the books she suggested – narratives by physicians analyzing their own practices – are unavailable in European academic libraries, and others have required some time to track down. I have been surprised to discover that in the United States, this literary genre appeals to a broad segment of the general public – a phenomenon that has no parallel in Europe, where this type of literature circulates in a much more restricted and scholarly arena (see, for example Klass 1987, Konner 1988, Hilfiker 1985, 2003, Verghese 1994, Campo 1998, Gawande 2003, Helman 2004).

[20] "Never perform in the presence of a layman; there is no religion without mystery". Jean-Marie-Placide Munaret (1805-1877) was a French country doctor who was eventually named a member of the Académie de Medecine.

[21] In a standard online search in Pub Med, I found a first reference in 1981 and an impressive increase since 2000.

complish your appointed destiny [...] and if he do not always come out of the combat with the words of triumph inscribed upon his banner, he has the consolation to know, if he has faithfully discharged his duty, that he has done all that human skill could devise, or human sagacity suggest." (Gross 1875: 7f.).

The expectation of success promoted by the hegemony of biomedicine is a long way from Gross' scepticism. In these early writings by doctors, we can find an antecedent to the modern "burnout syndrome": corrupt practice. Today the quality of medical practice is believed to be generally high, and the discomfort of professionals is expressed in terms of a "syndrome" or "disease", a metaphor that conveys the unease of professionals working in medical organizations that appear to ignore their professional and personal commitment to their calling. Perhaps "burnout syndrome" should be considered a work-related illness covered by insurance.

Health professionals locate the origins of this syndrome in the distance between the professional identity they internalised during their medical education, and their patients' demands. For their part, patients are increasingly dissatisfied with physicians they perceive as distant and uncommunicative. In the United States conflicts between patients and doctors are often resolved by recourse to the legal system; in Europe this tends not to be the case except in very extreme situations. However, as medical practice varies from one country to another, "burnout syndrome" or other symptoms of professional dissatisfaction may not reflect the same feelings everywhere. Here is a mid-19th century diagnosis from the U.S.:

"We are annoyed by unreasonable expectations and strange perverseness on the part of patients, and tormented by the inquisitiveness of their friends. Then we are forced to maintain a firm and tranquil demeanour when we are tortured with anxiety; to seem decided and confident in order that we may impart confidence, when we are distracted by doubt and uncertainty; and to appear cheerful when we are depressed by witnessing suffering and distress, and the defeat of our best endeavours." (Ware 1851: 20).

In Roman times, however, Pliny wrote of Greek physicians:

"They are a most wicked sort […] as soon as [Greece] manages to impose its literature on Rome, it will corrupt everything, and all the sooner if they manage to send us their doctors. They are plotting, in effect, to murder all barbarians with their medicine: a profession they practice for profit, in order to gain our trust and get rid of us more easily. Have no dealings with doctors!" (Pliny, Nat. History, cited in Kee 1992: 19).

Novels, plays, pamphlets, letters and other documents attack the venality, quackery, ignorance, and incompetence of medical practice. The acuteness of this criticism, as in Molière's *Malade imaginaire* portrayal of physicians as quacks or the Doctor Sangrado character in *Gil Blas* (Lesage 1980), expresses societal perceptions. Doctors do not ignore them:

"It has been a very common assertion, especially in late years, that the medical profession is not what it was in former times; that is less respectable, less cultured, less refined, less competent. In other words the great publics, sitting in judgement upon us, has declared that our ranks are overrun by all kind of loafers and self-styled doctors."(Gross 1875: 9).

The Hippocratic treatises (Hipócrates de Cos 1986) were full of recommendations about the attitude, the professional skill and the special sensitivity doctors should demonstrate before their patients, and explanations of physicians' obligations and medical ethics. The recovery of the Hippocratic texts in the late 17th century prompted new strategies of legitimating himselves for medical doctors in most European countries[22]. In order to compete successfully in a pluralistic health care market, doctors needed to improve their professional image. Accordingly, they began to introduce changes in medical education aimed at raising standards of clinical practice[23], devise new corporate strategies presenting doctors and pharmacists as apostles of modernity and science, engage in political lobbying and developing codes of ethics, and create narratives that define an ideal type of "good doctor". However, neither codes of ethics nor these narratives of good medical practice explain what doctors *do*; they show what doctors *must do* (Comelles 1998). Bad medical practice – and thus failure to maintain a proper professional attitude – was then seen not as the result of an illness, the sort of compassion fatigue we now call "burnout", but as a violation of an ethical principle. In that historical and cultural context, doctors attempted to develop a professional ethics in order to combat quackery, and one of the aims of medical training was to transform the professional into an academic and a humanist. In contempo-

---

[22] In Spain the effort to establish professional legitimacy is very old. In the late 13th century, the city of Valencia instituted an examination for doctors who wanted to work in the city (García Ballester, McVaughn & Rubio Vela 1989). A century later, the Protomedicato, an institution of professional legitimation, spread from Aragon to the kingdom of Castile. For more on this institution, see the dossier in Volume 16 of the journal *Dynamis* (López Terrada & Martínez Vidal (1996).

[23] See Risse (1999) on changes in medical education and the development of clinics, and von Bueltzingsloewen (1997) on the links between new experiments in medical education, the development of a new medical market and the articulation between doctors and the state in the pre-imperial Germany of the 18th and 19th centuries.

rary medical education, however, humanistic training is minimal, or rendered irrelevant by the need to acquire the specialized technical skills of the professional with some exceptions.

This is one of the lessons Konner (1988), an anthropologist who decided to study medicine, learned as a student at Harvard Medical School. Ten years older than most of his classmates, he was more aware of the fatigue that is so famously part of medical education, but experiencing it also gave him an important insight into how doctors learn to practice medicine and what role their own emotions play in patient care and medical decision-making. Fatigue, he argues, not only dulls your capacity for empathy; it makes you actively dislike the patient who spikes a fever or goes into cardiac arrest at three o'clock in the morning and requires your immediate and complete attention, when you have already been working for 48 hours on only three or four hours of sleep. And that dislike, Konner says, is actually necessary in order to be able to make life and death decisions about patients you have never met or had time to consult about their wishes. Fatigue, he concludes, is not merely an unfortunate consequence of the intensity of medical school; it is a pedagogical tool deliberately deployed in the service of medical education as training for scientific and technical competence. Other authors, however, such as Hilfiker (1985) Verghese (1994) and Campo (1998) have, on the basis of their own experiences, come to quite different conclusions about medical practice and the role of physicians' emotional connections to their profession and their patients[24].

I have been able to locate few contemporary sources in which modern physicians analyze their everyday practice[25], but I have found dozens of documents from different Western countries – most of them academic lectures, and a few books – in which doctors of the past used "good practice" as a kind of mirror, a way of focusing a critical gaze on what they considered "bad practices" in order to improve them. Their relevance, in my opinion, is the role these documents play in the social and cultural construction of a new

[24] These references were recommended to me by Susan DiGiacomo, who alerted me to the existence of a growing literary genre of autobiographical writing by physicians who can sometimes be quite critical of their own profession. See note 1.

[25] In the European languages I am able to read – the Romance languages and English – this type of autobiographical writing by physicians is less common and adopts a tone distinct from its American counterpart. Some are written as memoirs, like the two excellent volumes by the Catalan physician Broggi (2001, 2005), while others are purely anecdotal, and still others are diaries or reflective writings with a strongly philosophical streak. See also the French dossier in Galam (1996) about medical practice in France.

professional legitimacy in the context of forms of medical education and practice that enlarge the distance between the professionals, the patients and their relatives (Rosenberg 1992, Risse 1999).

My hypothesis is that this ideal type of the "good doctor" who empathizes with his patients is a social and cultural construction in contradiction with the new values of medical education, a contradiction that is the source of the current discontent of health professionals who experience daily the widening distance between the "good doctor" construct and the realities of contemporary medical practice. In Western and Northern European societies, to this situation should be added the change of status of physicians employed as civil servants at salaries far below those earned by their North American counterparts and in very different working conditions. In the remainder of this essay, I want to explore this contradiction by juxtaposing written narratives and visual narratives of medical practice: primarily photographs, but also some images drawn from television shows.

## Birth of the clinic, death of feelings?

Foucault's theory of the production of medical knowledge and power, developed in the early 1960s in a context of growing dissatisfaction after more than a decade of universal health coverage in the European welfare state, is very useful in explaining general trends in contemporary medical practice and health policy. Following the publication of *Birth of the clinic* (1978), his work met with generally uncritical acceptance[26]. In French history, as Castel (1976) and Goldstein (1997) have shown, doctors played an important role in the shaping of the Republic, achieving powerful positions as notables in local and state administration, in the control of health institutions and as corporate lobbyists. Historical evidence, however, shows that the relationship between the medical profession and the state evolved differently in Germany (von Bueltzingsloewen 1997) and Spain (Comelles 1988, 1991).

The *Birth of the clinic* traced the process through which patients became reified as the passive objects of medical knowledge, and their narratives, emotions and feelings lost their former importance as the source of physicians' ability to diagnose illness: "only observation and experience will set

[26] Recently some authors have taken exception to the centrality of Paris in the work of Foucault (1978) and also of Ackerknecht (1986). Both von Bueltzinsgloewen (1997) and Risse (1999) place the birth of the clinic in a larger European context.

medicine on a solid foundation" (Schmidtmann 1804 quoted in von Bueltzinsgsloewen 1997: 113).

However, the same 19th-century doctors who promoted sweeping changes in medical education also concerned themselves with the moral and ethical aspects of doctors' relationships with their clients.

"Sublime and holy is the doctor's mission [...] God has made you priest of the sacred fire of life and constituted you as the provider of the most beautiful gifts, those of life and health; he has entrusted you with the forces that lie hidden in nature so that you will use them for the benefit of your fellow men. Discharge your duty well, not for renown but for the Glory of God and for your brothers." (Hufeland quoted in Balaguer 1865: 23).

"[Doctors] must work tactfully and in a kindly way. [...] Young doctors must not forget that they need [poor] sick people if they are to attain the medical knowledge they need for their future professional life" (Hasse 1893 quoted in von Bueltzingsloewen 1997: 183)

Historical work by von Bueltzinsloewen (1997) and Risse (1999) on hospitals and changes in medical education and practice reveals a complex reality with idiosyncratic features in different countries. The so-called "medical model" emanating from Paris and from a changing German medical system took several decades to become hegemonic in the Western world[27]. Even today the most common form of medical practice, primary health care, is closer to patterns common at the beginning of the 20th century than to the forms of practice that predominate in big hospitals.

This is not to deny the hegemony of a medical model characterized by its biological reductionism, asocial gaze, pragmatic efficacy, anti-historicism and mercantilism (see Menéndez 1978, 1990). In any case, the hegemonic medical model is not monolithic but diverse because it has adapted to cultural processes, to local variations in scientific discourse, to specific processes of medical specialization, and to widely differing political strategies used to promote it. To maintain its hegemony, the medical model has developed subaltern fields not only in medical knowledge and practice, but also within the corporate group of health professionals: for example, homeopathy, or even, in my opinion, the field of primary health care in its enormous variety.

[27] The Flexner Report of 1915 – 80 years after the Paris school – was a major milestone in the transition to the new model in the United States (see Vogel 1980,1989, and Rosenberg 1986).

Although this entire corporate group shares a common model of medical education established by international conventions, differences arise at the local level in the variability of educational profiles in different countries or schools of medicine. For instance, the integration of the social sciences into medical school curricula in Europe is less developed than in American countries. In the opinion of Arthur Kleinman (1996 pers. com.), this marginal presence will do little to make medical graduates more sensitive to cultural or social diversity, or increase the value they place on patient narratives as opposed to clinical observation and reliance on technologically based diagnosis.

The displacement of patient narratives (anamnesis) to a subaltern position in the contemporary production of medical knowledge[28] is also a consequence of the changes in the patient-doctor encounter promoted by 18th-century reforms in clinical education. Prior to this time, the clinical encounter took place largely at the patients' bedside, in the margins of domestic space. The physician's presence was an intrusion into that space, and the encounter was managed through shared feelings and emotions. Let us look at two graphic examples of this shift.

In collections of 17th century Dutch paintings, there are dozens showing doctors, patients and members of the patient's family in bedside contexts[29]. The composition of these paintings is highly conventionalised: the patient is seated in an armchair, the relatives stand nearby, and the doctor scrutinizes a glass filled with urine. These scenes are static rather than dramatic, and do not depict emotions: what is being portrayed is the idea of technical competence. All the scenes are domestic, but the doctor is someone "different," dressed in a black suit.

The birth of the clinic introduces a crucial change. The clinic removed patients from domestic space, confining them in hospitals in order to produce medical knowledge. In this institutional context, patients become "the other" in a space controlled by doctors. Rows of beds placed along the walls of the hospital ward construct a specific space of knowledge. The features of participant observation that were present in the doctor'spractice at the bedside of the patient have disappeared, and the processes of transference and

[28] For more on the history of medical anamnesis, see the classic work by Laín Entralgo (1998).

[29] Some Internet portals provide access to a wealth of materials. See, for example, the Spanish *Fisterra*, which contains a guide to literary documents on medicine and a virtual exhibition of paintings on medical themes (http://www.fisterra.com/human/index.asp).

counter-transference between doctors, patients and the patient's relatives were irrevocably altered by this shift.

In the pictures of hospital wards at the beginning of the 20th century, physicians appear hieratic, standing close to the seated patient as in old Dutch paintings. The patient's relatives, however, have disappeared. There is no suffering, no emotions, and no feelings. The main idea is modernity and efficacy and was intended to publicize the institution and attract charitable donations, and the photographer needed a scene that would move the viewer to generosity. A century earlier, a printed image of Laënnec examining a patient with a stethoscope recalls the scenes depicted by Dutch painters. Seated at the patient's bedside in the hospital ward, Laënnec listens to his lungs, but looks in the direction of his colleagues and the nurses standing in the foreground. No emotions are present, only knowledge. It illustrates the evolution from the domestic scene to the birth of the clinic, a transition marked by changes in medical education and the construction of a discourse on medico-scientific competence.

The paradox is that the Laënnec illustration was not the rule but the exception in 19th and early 20th century medical practice. The generalization of the new medicine required the establishment of diagnostic and therapeutic hospitals that became widespread in western societies in the mid- 20th century, a process that accelerated only after World War II. Before the war and the role played by antibiotics in shaping internal medicine in the late 1950s (Comelles 2004), the discourse defending changes in medical education on the grounds of diagnostic efficacy was largely an attempt to discredit quackery, folk healers and domestic medicine (Comelles 1996, 2000). There was tremendous competition between quacks, apothecaries, pharmacists, doctors, and folk healers because they all worked in the same domestic market[30]. Some paintings illustrate a very common case: doctor, a priest, and the relatives surround the patient, all playing complementary roles. However, the doctor was called in critical situations, sometimes as a last resort, in a context of massive use of domestic medicine[31]. Ease of access to doctors was one of the more important demands of the working class.

---

[30] A very good description of the relationships between doctors and folk healers in Enlightenment Spain can be found in Perdiguero (1997).

[31] See Gelfand (1981) on France; Porter & Porter (1989) on England, Zarzoso (2001) on the case of Barcelona (Spain). For an account of medical pluralism in the 18th century see Perdiguero (2002) and the dossier in the journal *Dynamis* edited by Ballester, López Terrada & Martínez Vidal (2002).

## The corporate reinvention of an empathic medical role

Jean-Marie Placide Munaret (1805-1877) was a rural practitioner in 19th century France, but hardly a simple country doctor[32]. He learned medicine in Paris during "the birth of the clinic" and later obtained his Ph.D. in Montpellier. He became a *notable* during the Second Empire, and was a member of the Academy of Medicine. He had a lively interest in both literature and art, amassing a library of some 20,000 volumes and a large collection of paintings of doctors. Borrowing the title of the novel by Balzac, he published a manual, *Du Médecin des villes et du medecin de campagne* (Munaret 1840), in which he tried to explain the specificities of rural medical practice in France to young doctors. The book combines a narrative of his experience as a "practical doctor" in a peasant milieu with a treatise on common diseases and extensive comments and insights about the best way to work in and adapt to a rural context about which nothing is taught in hospitals and schools of medicine:

"It is true that, having spent years trailing through hospital wards in the wake of a professor who teaches him to see only what he himself sees, or wants to see, a young doctor starts his professional life, whether in town or in the country, unaware that in either place he will always be required to demonstrate, in his practice as well as in his manners, that inherent distinction which separates the pale-skinned, mellifluous, impressionable city dweller from the sturdy rustic with his dark complexion and rough hands, whom nothing impresses, wounds, or tires." (Munaret 1840: IX).

A century later a young Mexican *pasante*[33] wrote:

"During our university education we learn a reality very far removed from rural life. In that milieu, the *pasante* is alone, without the help of his professors, armed only with basic knowledge that allows him a limited ability to act, and exposes him to the possibility of serious error. In those very difficult conditions the *pasante* needs to develop an awareness of his responsibility to his patients." (Velázquez 1987: 1)

Between the 19th-century French countryside and rural Mexico there was no essential difference. I can even find parallels between the behaviour of British urban practitioners after World War II (see Helman 1978) and the auto-

---

[32] http://www.academie-medecine.fr/bibliotheque/bibliotheque6.asp#munaret

[33] In Mexico, the *pasante* is a doctor sent to perform a year of civil service practicing medicine in the rural *rancherías* following graduation from medical school. The *pasantía* program began in 1937 under the left-wing government of Lorenzo Cárdenas.

biographies of Catalan rural doctors published in the second half of the 20th century (Danés 1978, Pla 2000). Even quite recent descriptions of rural practice show considerable continuity with earlier ones:

"... he has a special scent. He is rugged, bushy, and gentle all at the same time, wears heavy corduroy and makes precise gestures, is occasionally brutal or grumpy, but so effective [...] he is forgiven anything but absence [...] Ah, life! Medical practice at a distance from the tools of science and university hospitals allows me to take an interest in the real reasons that lead patients to consult me." (Galam 1996: 66-67) "I work as well as I can, blocked by the uncertainty of my role and my position. I practice a minimal kind of medicine. My basic rule is not to reject my patients when they seek my help for something non-medical." (Galam 1996: 81)

The continuity between Munaret's writings and the experience of modern physicians is evidence for the existence of a subaltern model within the current hegemonic medical model. All these writers note the distance between what is taught in schools of medicine, and the lifeworlds they encounter outside medical school, at the bedside of their patients[34]. The bedside encounter is a fundamental part of medical practice. We cannot conceive of biomedicine without it; yet contemporary medicine is represented in images of hospital wards, ICU's and emergency services, and operating rooms. The continuity and persistence of representations of the ideal type – the image of the "good old-fashioned doctor" – requires explanation.

In 1849 a senior professor, John Ware, delivered a lecture to the medical students at Harvard Medical School on the *Duties and qualifications of physicians*:

"No man ought to meet with great success in the practice of medicine, unless he be actually well informed – unless he deserve it. And few do reach to a truly desirable kind of height of reputation without being well educated, fail in attaining to such a reputation, and find themselves, through life, far behind many contemporaries who have not half their talents or medical knowledge. A physician must have other accomplishments than those, which are strictly professional. His relation to society is something more than that of a mere investigator of the character of disease and a dispenser of the means of curing it he must have other qualifications. It is true you have no immediate use for the qualifications of which I speak. Having no direct personal connection

[34] One of the best documents is the French novel *La maladie de Sachs* by Winckler (1998). The author, a doctor, tells the story of a primary care physician in a rural part of contemporary France. I believe it is one of the best ethnographic depictions of medical practice even if the plot is fictional.

with patients, you cannot exercise the accomplishment to which I refer." (Ware 1849: 2).

On March 11, 1875, Samuel Gross, a professor of surgery, gave *The valedictory address delivered at the Philadelphia Academic of Music before the trustees, faculty and students of the Jefferson Medical College at his 49th Annual Commencement* on the subject of *The glory and the hardships of the medical life.*

"Many persons imagine that the physician is omnipotent, and therefore, capable of performing miracles, forgetting that it is appointed unto all men once to die. A highly educated, enlightened and skilful physician is at once the ornament of his profession, and a prince among men. He yields to no man, or class of men, in point of dignity in real greatness, or in his power of doing good. Many of the dearest interests of the community in which he lives are daily entrusted to his keeping." (Gross 1875: 8ff.).

To play this role, the physician ought to be the patient's steadfast friend.

"In time of epidemics each house became a hospital. [The doctor] hears only the voice of duty that calls him to the homes of twenty families, poor or rich. He is equally solicitous to all without distinctions; he grieves with them and comforts them in spite of the distance, the weather and the darkness. Occupied always by the suffering of others, he forgets his own." (Munaret 1840: 48).

A well known painting by Sir Luke Fields (Tate Gallery, London)[35] shows the physician in an attitude Gross and Munaret would have recognized and approved of. The distance between this and the 17th century Dutch pictorial genre is enormous: here the doctor sits, worried, at the bedside of a sick child, in a working-class home; the father is a shadow standing stoically in the background while the child's mother weeps in desperation. The artist gives us an emotional drama, and clues to the doctor's role:

"But even in the supposition that medicine is of no efficacy in the way commonly supposed, still, with the present belief and feelings of mankind on the subject, the profession would be of incalculable value as a benevolent institution for alleviating the anxieties and assuming the responsibility of sickness." (Ware 1849: 13f.).

[35] *The Doctor* (1891) by Sir Luke Fields, Tate Gallery, London.

The lectures by Ware and Gross were concerned with duties. Munaret suggests going to the field and becoming "one of them". I believe that Littré's[36] narrative about his experience shows how thoroughly internalised this model was at the highest level of the profession:

"I practiced very little medicine; but for two decades, in my village I was able to offer my peasant neighbours some care. Since I was careful and sufficiently well trained, I was certainly useful to them, and for that usefulness I obtained the best of all possible rewards: their recognition, manifested in a constant good will and, when I needed it, their help. There I discovered how much anguish medicine might cause, when in serious cases where the patient's life is at stake, uncertainty about the diagnosis or treatment and the fear of making a mistake are a source of torment and even shame. The doctor's responsibility and his power are all out of proportion to one another; one is great, while the other is small; and it is precisely because of the limits of his power that the loss of even a small portion of it causes great anxiety [...] Another source of pain in the practice of medicine is the ability to foresee events; not for oneself, for I have seen more than one doctor recognize in himself the signs of incurable illness and, long in advance of the fact, pronounce upon himself the death sentence of which any other would have remained unaware until the very end; the pain is not for himself, but for those he cares about whose lives are threatened by illness. This foresight is a form of torture the doctor tries to spare his patients, but when he can no longer maintain for them the illusion of hope by preserving their ignorance, the weeks, months and years grow long indeed." (Littré 1875: V).

There is no doubt that all these writers are skilled and "modern" doctors at the intellectual pinnacle of their profession. Ware and Gross are professors in important universities, Littré a great scholar, Munaret a member of the French medical academy and author of a great many books and articles. Their point of departure was the Hippocratic texts taught in schools of medicine; these works inspired their codes of ethics. However, the reasons for developing this ideal model were grounded in religious or philanthropic discourses. It was also a strategy for developing a market, and for influencing the lower classes, both peasants and workers.

"And I say further, my friend; (the doctor) must be able to converse easily with peasants and shake hands, in a dignified and cordial way, with the householder who greets him or takes leave of him; and in the same way he

---

[36] Littré, a doctor and philologist, was also the translator of the *Corpus Hippocraticum*.

must not decline the frugal hospitality that awaits him at the end of a long and arduous journey. Seated at a wobbly table close to a rustic hearth, the doctor may take advantage of the opportunity to offer his wisdom to these good people, instructing them as they sit silently grouped around him. Oh, it is then that the ministry of the country doctor is sublime …" (Munaret 1840: 39)

The relationship of trust between doctors, patients and patients' relatives requires that doctors learn to be sympathetic to their patients' distress, based on their field experience. As in Hippocratic texts, doctors are urged to combine participant observation inside patients' homes with a respectful attitude and display of professional skill.

"The peasant is curious, inquisitive even with his doctor; he wants to know the name and the history of the illness for which he has consulted you. Hasten to respond to him and to make yourself understood, for the art of making oneself intelligible applies to all things, according to M.A. Petit; and since it is one of the best means of persuasion, it must be one of the first things a doctor learns. If it is a case of gastroenteritis, for example, tell him that it is an inflammation of the stomach and bowels; in the same way, justify the treatment used, and when you finish do not forget to add that doctors call this illness *gastroenteritis*." (Munaret 1840: 40).

"Be careful", warned Munaret, "otherwise, if you maintain the laconicism characteristic of city life…you will hardly have crossed the threshold of a peasant hut when all the relatives will start in on you: *Not very impressive, is he, this doctor, he has no idea what to say*.... And the very same day you will be invited not to return unless they send word for you to come, because *the patient is better*. In less diplomatic terms: because you didn't know how to win their confidence, some cleverer and more loquacious colleague has taken your place" (Munaret 1840: 40).

Munaret was a keen observer of interactions in rural homes between doctors and householders. I see in his writing a genuine effort to establish analytic distance from the scene he wanted to depict. Munaret's irony adds ethnographic value to his observations. Ware, in his lecture, developed a fine analysis of the conflicts occasioned by the doctor's lack of comprehension:

"We are apt to complain of the unreasonableness of patients and their friends, and we perhaps suffer ourselves too often to be betrayed into expressions of irritation and disgust at what appears to be an ungrateful and unfounded want of confidence on their part, though it really is not meant as such. We are not always so considerate in these cases as the circumstances demand. We do not make allowance enough for the effects produced by sickness in mind." (Ware 1849: 20f.).

This is a good description of the effects of transference and counter-transference, concepts that psychoanalysis would develop at the end of the 19th century. There is no irony here. Samuel Gross, in his lecture, focuses on the development of a professional work ethic as the key to successful medical practice because he is, like Ware, speaking to students and not to colleagues as Munaret did:

"The physician qualifies himself for his arduous duties by hard work and long-continued efforts. It is by no sudden inspiration of genius that he can diagnosticate disease, penetrate the secrets of nature, or successfully cope with disease and death. Long days and nights of patient labour alone can qualify him for the discharge of the great functions of his office" (Gross 1875: 11)

All these documents, as well as others I found as lectures in the *Academia de medicina y cirugía de Barcelona*, relate to the need for professional legitimation in the context of a growing general awareness of doctors' power. As Gross wrote:

"The sick, the halt, the blind and the deaf in every direction, far and near are attracted to him, and he virtually holds in his hands the keys of health, of life, and of death. There is literally no end to his power of doing good; like a magician, he says to disease, thus far shall thou go and no further; to pain and anguish, be still; to sleep, return to the wearied eye; to the oppressed and delirious brain, throw off your phantasies and resume your empire." (Gross 1875: 11f.)

Through this double commitment, both scientific and social, the "good doctor" plays a role akin to that of priest and "at the heart of the storm, of the labyrinth of dissolution, of illness and death [...] who can save society? Who can show it the path it should take and light its way, as Moses did for the People of Israel? Who? Two men scorned by society and denied recognition because they will not flatter her, and whom she regards with contempt because they do not cease to serve her. These two stand at the doorway to life, and walk together to the edge of the grave, receiving man at birth, accompanying and guiding him along the road of time, and never abandoning him until he reaches the threshold of eternity. This is a universal law in the civilized world, at least in the Catholic world. I think you can guess that I am speaking of the priest and the physician." (Balaguer 1865: 21f.).

Munaret, skeptical of this kind of religious excess, describes in a more secular language the medical practitioner's role in the new society:

"As an apostle of civilization, he instructs the peasants in their reciprocal obligations: of father to child, of citizen to state, of the heart to the sweet bond of the family, of the soul to its fate; he shakes with a prudent hand the trunk of certain prejudices concerning health, and when it is sufficiently loosened, he firmly uproots it; he points out harmful habits and the superstitions that surround them...and if from the good seed he sows in the as yet uncultivated field of their intelligence there grow any shafts of wheat worth harvesting, that is his reward." (Munaret 1840: 39).

In contrast to these lofty aims, we can also find more down-to earth assessments of the doctor'simage and role in society. It is easy to read them as cynical; I prefer to see them as a reflection of the contradictions present in this idealization of the physician's role:

"A diligent attention to business soon runs up [a doctor's] reputation for diligence, like a fast-growing wine, that under its shadow, if he is so disposed he can loiter at leisure. If the sound of the mortar is heard in the room, it makes little difference whether he is grinding spices for his landlady's accommodation, or powders for his pills. Seen dimly through his window shades poring over a book, they say that he is studious, and his fame rises, and it is all the same whether the volume he reads is Bulwer or Broussais, Dickens or Dewes, Cowper or Cooper. Seen writing at his desk, he gains credit at once for an intelligent student, possibly for an author, and it all the same whether he is making his sparse receipts equal the bill of his expenses upon the balance-sheet, noting his cases, or writing a tale for some literary Monthly. Lucky blunders will be construed to his credit" (Tuthill 1855: 9).

Tuthill's unflattering portrait suggests to me (Comelles 1998) that the ideal type of good medical practice was constructed on empirically weak foundations. What was the aim behind Ware's and Gross' lectures? Were they only recommendations to students, or part of an attempt to raise the standard of practice? I am not sure. There are few ethnographic accounts of medical practice, and historians have had difficulty locating reports documenting the practices of the past. The absence of such reports may be the result of an absence of professional consensus on the rules of medical practice. Munaret (1840: 8) suggests something of this kind when he blames a lack of ethics and public regulation of medical services for the existence of bad medical practices. To his colleagues he suggested, ironically, an extreme solution that probably would have pleased Balzac:

"There is only one way left for you to keep your clients, my friend, but it is an extreme resort: get married, find a wife with a fine property where you may grow the wheat for your table, and with a big family that will help to establish you firmly in the area." (Munaret 1840: 18f.)

## From medical pluralism to the bilateral doctor-patient relationship

During the 20th century, hundred of papers were published analysing the doctor-patient relationship and the roles of patients and doctors. Most of them convert the ideal type of the good doctor involved in complex relationships with his patients, their families, and their lifeworlds to a much simpler model, that of the dyadic patient-doctor relationship. This process is directly traceable to the development of the medical model and the subsequent reification of the patient, the exclusion of social and cultural context as a source of explanation, and the progressive marginalization of the role of the patient's social network in health-seeking behaviour. The dyadic doctor/patient relationship is the outcome of the interaction of several factors: the medical appropriation of patients' bodies in clinics and hospitals; the development of a new strategy for marketing medical services (the doctor's office); the influence of psychoanalysis and psychotherapeutic discourse; and the influence of such authors as Parsons (1984) in the United States, intellectuals such as Binswanger or von Weizsäcker in Germany, or Laín Entralgo (1964).

The intellectual aim of the Europeans was not to develop a theoretical debate within the social sciences about the medical practice[37], but to address issues arising from the development of the European welfare state[38], most of which had to do with professional socialization. The European discourse was rooted in philosophical schools like phenomenology, in contrast to the influences of the empiricism and positivism of American sociologists such as Parsons. In Spain and Latin America, the work of Laín Entralgo (1908-2001), a Spanish historian of medicine and philosopher, exerted a powerful influence for almost four decades. Laín's writings were largely oriented toward developing a "medical anthropology"[39] closely related to the German

[37] This is, however, the case for authors such as Parsons (1984) or Freidson (1978).

[38] Even Fabrega (1974) wrote from a medical perspective. This was not, however, true of the concept of folk medicine in Black's (1883) work.

[39] Laín had a very prominent intellectual position during the Franco dictatorship. He wrote political and ideological essays and remained on good terms with the regime even though his thinking shifted towards

"Medizinanthropologie" and the Dutch "Medische Antropologie"[40], whose intellectual roots lie in the work and the German philosophers like Husserl, Scheler or Heidegger, and in Roman Catholic philosophers like the Spanish Zubiri. Laín argued for an ideal model of the doctor linked to the ideals of Hippocratic ethics, a notion of the patient-doctor relationship based on an intellectual friendship: the patient, seeking treatment for his illness, finds a friend in his doctor. This theory is developed in Laín's seminal book *La relación médico-enfermo* (Laín Entralgo 1964), in a later work *Antropología médica* (1984) and dozens of other books and papers. He believed (Laín Entralgo 1984: 19f.) that the magical mentality (a pre-scientific one) and the technical mentality (the scientific one) have the same effect: to separate the patient physically from the doctor, and to render useless the personal encounter between them.

The Hippocratic model of practice (Laín Entralgo 1987), however, had already been abandoned by biomedicine, and the socialization of medicine in Europe – including Spain under the Franco regime – was well established. The idealized intellectual and emotional patient-doctor relationship was not an empirical reality in medical practice, except for the educated sectors of the upper middle class and the bourgeoisie. Laín was aware of Parsons' work on the sick role, but did not undertake any empirical research of his own in order to support his position with ethnographic evidence. His work sought instead to develop good practices on the basis of an ethical discourse grounded in Roman Catholic charity. Although Laín Entralgo was a doctor, he never had a clinical practice. His positions resemble those of Ware, Gross or Munaret, but with an important difference: they were practicing physicians of an earlier time whose writings were grounded in their experience, while Laín was a 20th century intellectual, an armchair theoretician of medical practice who did not realize that the model he advocated was incompatible with the realities of modern medical systems in Europe and Latin America except in the highly restricted context of private medicine for the upper classes. He was popular among the enemies of the socialization of medicine as a source of arguments in favor of private practice and against the welfare state. His hostility to the technical evolution of medicine placed him outside the arena of hospital care, where his work is of highly limited applicability. For doctors working in hospital wards, Laín's discourse makes little sense.

more democratic ideas in the 1960s; see his autobiography (Laín Entralgo 1976). For further information on his political and intellectual role, see Moran (1998).

40 See Diasio's (1999) monograph on the origins of medical anthropology in several European countries (the United Kingdom, France, Italy and the Netherlands).

A comparative reading of Laín's works and Parsons' analysis of the sick role reveals points of similarity that might have made it possible to construct a theory of the "good doctor" based on field observation. Parsons' writings generated debate among social scientists, and became one of the points of departure for the sociology of medicine and medical anthropology, but ultimately did not lead either to the production of a discourse on good medical practice, or to revision of the "good doctor" ideal type. Laín remains a figure significantly out of touch with his own time, and his defense of an intellectual and affective bond between doctor and patient is an ethical discourse of very limited applicability to the context of the modern hospital. Up to this point, we have examined narratives by doctors for an audience of doctors. I now turn to the popularisation of these narratives for a wider audience.

## The good doctor in the media world

Fifty years after the publication of the Flexner Report, the television show *Marcus Welby, M.D.* became one of the most popular programs in the United States, achieving an audience share of 25 percent. The main character was a general practitioner in his fifties, Marcus Welby (played by Robert Young), with a private office in a middle-class neighbourhood, and a handsome young practitioner as his partner[41]. The enthusiasm with which the American public embraced *Marcus Welby, M.D.* was not a new phenomenon in the United States. Turow's (1988) study of films and television shows demonstrates that media interest in medical subjects begins in the 1930s with film, but starting in the 1950s, with the growth in television audiences, television programs about doctors began to displace cinematic representations. Focusing on shows aired in the US between the mid-fifties and the mid-eighties, he demonstrates an intimate relationship between the media and professional associations such as the American Medical Association (AMA), and traces changing perspectives on the medical profession through different shows. I do not have space here for a detailed analysis of all television programs in this genre, which is much more firmly established in the United States than in Europe. European television channels have purchased some of these shows for broadcast here, but by no means all, and audience responses have

---

[41] See http://www.museum.tv/archives/etv/M/htmlM/marcuswelby/marcuswelby.htm. (Visited August 2, 2004). There is an extensive description of the program and audience responses to it. It was aired in the US between September 1969 and May 1976, and in Spain in the early 1970s.

been uneven[42]. An important factor in the reception of American doctor shows is the difference between European and American health care systems[43]. I have no doubt, and Turow's book supports this perception, that American medical associations were quick to grasp the positive impact these series could have on doctors' professional image, and they played a significant consulting role in the creation of characters and the content of scripts.

In two recent articles, Flores (2002, 2004) reviews 131 feature films from nine countries for their depiction of doctors as main characters. The results of this study show that movie physicians are overwhelmingly white, male, and under 40 years of age. The proportion of female and minority film physicians has declined steadily in recent decades. They are commonly surgeons (33%), psychiatrists (26%), and family practitioners (18%) and in 44% of films they are portrayed negatively, a growing trend since the 1960s[44]. Physicians are frequently depicted as greedy, egotistical, uncaring, and unethical, especially in recent films. Medical inaccuracies occurred in 27% of the films studied. Compassion and idealism were common in early physician movies but are increasingly scarce in recent decades. A recurrent theme is the "mad scientist", the physician-researcher who values research more than his patients' welfare. Portrayals of physicians as egotistical and materialistic have increased, while sexism and racism have waned. Movies from the past two decades have explored critical issues surrounding medical ethics and managed care. Flores concludes that negative portraits of physicians are on the rise, and this may adversely affect patient expectations and the patient-physician relationship. He accepts, nevertheless, that films about physicians can serve as useful gauges of public opinion about the medical profession, as tools for medical education, and as instruments of positive social change in efforts to reform managed care.

---

[42] In Spain *Dr. Kildare, Dr. Gannon* and *Marcus Welby, MD* was the only American medical-themed series broadcast until 1980. More recently, broadcast of *St. Elsewhere* met with relative success in Catalonia. *ER* Emergency Room was a complete failure in Spain, while in France it was a media phenomenon. In Spain *Doctor In Alaska* enjoyed a modest degree of success.

[43] The case of *ER* in France was unique, since it opened a professional debate among physicians on the state of emergency medicine in France. In certain respects the organization of French hospitals resembles that of American public hospitals, and they sell their services to the public health care administration.

[44] In television, by contrast, the trend is to portray physicians as main characters in a positive light. In feature films made by independent producers or in European films, there is greater freedom to depict situations of conflict than in prime-time television, where large audiences of mainstream viewers are essential. Turow (1988) offers several examples. My own experience with television portrayals of doctors and medicine is limited to *Marcus Welby, Dr. Kildare, Medical Center, St Elsewere, Doctor in Alaska*, and *Emergency Room* (*ER*); two Spanish shows, *Urgencias* and *Médico de Familia*; and the Catalan docu-drama *Bellvitge Hospital.*

Film audiences are smaller than and different from those of television, and the more attractive image of medicine seen in television shows is probably a consequence of more stringent control of representations of doctors. Susan DiGiacomo (personal communication) notes that the series *Gideon's Crossing*, broadcast on the ABC network during 2000-2001, lasted less than one season. Set in a minimally disguised Massachusetts General Hospital, the series was inspired by a book by Jerome Groopman, MD. The stories were based on real cases, and the tension between the ideal image of the good doctor and the demands of practice in a research hospital was foregrounded. DiGiacomo believes that the series' failure resulted from the inability of the mass media to tolerate significant levels of ambiguity, nuance and complexity. By contrast, however, *ER*, a star-system series with a level of technical accuracy approaching the documentary, achieved consistently high ratings.

Turow's and Flores' work shows the extent to which the media have a leading role in the construction of cultural representations of the medical profession. In the U.S., the heavy pressure exerted on television producers by professional medical associations and the presence of medical advisors on the production staff are signs that for the first time, doctors are no longer independently constructing a discourse on medical practice. The paradox is that, at a time when the medical profession was engaged in establishing the hegemony of biomedicine, that very hegemony became an object of representation in which more was at stake than the corporate interests of doctors; the entire complex of political, economic, and cultural forces involved in the management of health care in the United States also had interests to protect. For this reason, when television networks began in the 1950s to shift the medical genre from cinema to the TV screen, the American Medical Association found it necessary to lobby the networks on its own behalf in order not to lose control over its own public image (Turow 1988). Since the early 1970s, the genre has diversified and includes not only the medical arena of the hospital but also general practitioners like Welby, although his function is not to treat cases of pneumonia but to attend to the social problems of his clients.

If we shift this issue to Spain, we see a different reality. Unlike the medical drama format of *ER* or *St. Elsewhere*, three of the most successful Spanish TV shows, *Farmacia de Guardia, Médico de familia*, and *Hospital General*, are more like medical soap operas, focusing not on the professional lives but on the sentimental lives of doctors and nurses. There are very few episodes dealing with medical practice, and in any case the medical profile is not that of a doctor practicing in a public hospital, despite fact that the vast majority of Spanish physicians work in the public health care system. While *Médico de familia* was enormously popular, *Marcus Welby, M.D.* failed to appeal to Spanish audiences, probably because the environment of Welby's practice in the U.S. was too remote from people's experience with family doctors in Spain. At the time of *Marcus Welby's* failure in Spain, two other American medical shows were enjoying significant success: *Dr. Kildare* and *Medical Center*. Richard Chamberlain and Chad Everett played two young, handsome and skilled doctors working in a modern hospital, treating diseases that required the mobilization of impressive technological resources. Their knowledge and skill were the source of the drama. In the United States, the uniform success of *Dr. Kildare, Medical Center,* and *Marcus Welby* may be the result of broad social acceptance of both the scientific competency model and the "good doctor" model of medical practice. In Spain, however, the great success of *Dr. Kildare* and *Medical Center* and the relative failure of *Marcus Welby*, all three of which were broadcast during approximately the same time period, may be traceable to the fact that at the time they were aired, Spanish hospitals were beginning a shift from public beneficent institutions to modern high-tech ones. It is possible that the image of a new kind of physician – handsome, young and technically skilled – better represented the aspirations of an emergent consumer society for which the image of the kindly and sympathetic general practitioner, whether rural or urban, had come to be associated with poverty, misery, and ignorance.

After the 1980s, once the Spanish social security system was fully in place, television shows on doctors and hospitals started to lose some of their former popularity. Spanish hospitals of today are no different technologically or organizationally than those represented in *St. Elsewhere* or *ER*, although often the situations and problems depicted in these American programs are unfamiliar to Spanish viewers or European viewers in general. For this reason, *ER*, despite its high quality and the Spielberg trademark, failed to catch on in Spain, while shows like *Farmacia de guardia, Médico de familia* and *Hospital Central*, which treated the world of medicine only as the backdrop for the main character's personal life, were very successful. Subsequently, the private channel Tele 5 broadcast *Hospital General*, a show with an ensemble cast, but one that interspersed the characters' romantic adventures with gory sequences verging on bad taste. With the single exception of *Bellvitge Hospital*, a docu-drama produced by Televisió de Catalunya and sponsored by the Catalan ministry of health[45], Spanish television shows have not been privileged sites for the construction of a discourse on medical practice.

This admittedly incomplete tour of media representations of medical practice suggests that during the last third of the 20th century, the American medical profession lost exclusive control of the construction of the image of the good doctor, and since then it has had to negotiate the content of this image with the mass media, which were, in turn, influenced by other social, cultural, and political forces. Doctor shows began to reflect to a greater extent the experience of patients and to a lesser extent the individualism and authoritarianism characteristic of former representations of medical practice. In the majority of television shows – and in many films – there is more space for the depiction of emotions and feelings, but in most cases, apart from the exceptions Flores identifies, the image of the good doctor continues to be presented, anachronistically, in much the same way as in the writings of the nineteenth-century authors quoted above. In an age of high-tech hospital-based medical practice, the contradictions inherent in this image of the good doctor destabilize it. As in Munaret's time, one response to dissonance is cynicism. The most recent doctor show, *House, M.D.* (Fox Network 2004), depicts a physician who is a brilliant diagnostician but has no interest in his patients.

## Epilogue

A recent web page, updated in 2002[46], says:

"If you don't remember, [Marcus Welby] was a family doctor on a television show. He was a friend and a counsellor and a problem solver. He and those who worked with him at his office cared for all kinds of patients in all kind of conditions, in the best and in the worst of times. Some of us were fortunate to have a Marcus Welby care for us when we were growing up.

Did you know that there are still Family Doctors in this nation, and even a number who would qualify for the world class Marcus Welby level? Not only are they out there, but they are better trained than ever.

---

[45] Produced as an experiment. The program never achieved a very large audience in part because it was too closely linked to the interests of the medical profession and for this reason lacked an independent critical vision of the health care system.

[46] This text is included in the University of Nebraska Medical Center webpage, in a section on rural medicine http://www.unmc.edu/Community/ruralmeded/marcus_welby.htm advocating improvement in the training of medical students for family practice in rural areas.

Did you know that two physicians who died in Desert Storm were family physicians? Family physicians are on the front lines in the military, in inner city urban areas, in rural areas, in the suburbs, everywhere. If we ever, God forbid, have future terrorist acts involving infection, family physicians will be on the front lines before the rest of the nation.

Did you know that Family Medicine doctors are the only doctors that serve in every location in the United States, including the smallest towns where no other doctors go?

Did you know that the US Government has continued over many years to waste billions trying to get more doctors to go to these towns, when all they had to do was choose the right students to go to medical school, ones who wanted to serve their patients, the ones most likely to choose Family Medicine? Did you know that these students were more likely to serve in rotations overseas, and in rural areas? Did you know that these students were more likely to volunteer to serve people in need even while busy learning about medicine?

Seems like serving others is a strong point about Family Medicine. It is a characteristic that you can identify in family physicians before, during, and after medical school and residency. It is also a strong point in physicians doing mental health, geriatrics, surgery, and obstetrics. Not surprisingly family physicians also take on these tasks, in addition to holding up the fine and honored tradition of General Practice.

Did you know that the numbers of medical students choosing family medicine are dropping rapidly? Did you know that top medical school leaders have recommended getting doctors who had broader characteristics, but medical schools continue to choose based primarily on intellectual scores on tests and grades in college? Not surprisingly we have fewer and fewer interested in serving, especially serving in underserved areas. We also have more and more medical schools interested in getting students who will become researchers. After all, the way medical schools get more dollars is by having more researchers, not by graduating doctors who leave medical schools and serve in other locations. Research demands a person with an inward focus, and ability to concentrate and immerse in concepts and data. Selecting for research means selecting away from service and involvement.

Do you think that this might be a reason why you have a hard time talking to your doctor anymore? Guess who leads medical schools in the fight to have students understand the importance of communicating with patients, or trying to prevent disease, or understanding how to serve the elderly, people from other cultures, those who have been abused, or people who are mired in poverty and ignorance?

*Medical schools need to know that you must have a doctor who at least attempts to understand you. Our nation needs doctors who work with schools and communities to help solve some of the complex problems that threaten to undermine our nation."*

I have quoted this web page at length because it illustrates the persistence of an ideal type of doctor despite its subaltern status. The questions raised by the authors of the University of Nebraska web page speak directly to the concerns of patients, and depict an arena of medical practice far from the expectations of the majority of medical students. I am not sure whether the Marcus Welby figure the web page promotes is at present the most common image of the ideal type of doctor. The modern counterparts of Ware and Gross would probably lecture their students on evidence-based medicine, and in Europe most medical students have never heard of Parsons or, for that matter, medical anthropology or the sociology of medicine. Most newly minted doctors, well trained in the institutional model of hospital practice, are at a loss to understand the inner-city slums, the poor rural communities, or for that matter the middle-class neighborhoods where they end up practicing after they graduate from medical school.

For Ware, Gross or Marcus Welby, the satisfactions of their professional lives were derived from the human and social dimensions of medical practice. Today, the professional reality many doctors encounter after their training does not meet this standard of expectation. The University of Nebraska web page proposes an alternative that would adjust medical training to meet the needs of poorly served sectors of society. In Spain, family physicians strive for a high standard of practice but often appear not to understand what it is their patients want from them, and they end up simply writing prescriptions. Perhaps, in a world of universal health coverage and bureaucratised medicine, "burnout syndrome" is not something only physicians experience, and the common ground on which patients and their doctors meet is that of disillusionment and a sense of lost possibility.

"There was a prudent grave Physician,
Careful of Patients as you'd wish one;
Much Good he did with Purge and Glister,

And well he knew to raise a Blister;
Many he cur'd, and more he wou'd,
By Vomit, Flux, and letting Blood;
But still his Patients came again,
And most of their old Ills complain (...)".
(Anonymous Scottish broadside ballad, circa 1700-1720: An Account of the Doctor and his Patients)[47]

## References

Ackerknecht, E. H.
1986 [1967] *La médecine hospitalière a Paris (1794-1848).* Paris: Payot.

Balaguer, P.
1865 *De las funestas consecuencias fisicas y morales de la inobservancia de los preceptos higienicos en nuestra sociedad.* Discurso Inaugural 2 de enero de 1865. Barcelona: Academia de Medicina de Barcelona.

Ballester, R.; López Terrada, M. L.; Martínez Vidal, A.
2002 Monográfico: La realidad de la práctica médica: el pluralismo asistencial en la Monarquía Hispánica (ss.XVI-XVIII). *Dynamis* 22, Granada: Universidad de Granada.

Black, W. G.
1982 [1883] *Medicina popular. Un capítulo en la historia de la cultura.* Barcelona: Alta-Fulla.

[47] http://www.nls.uk/broadsides/broadside.cfm/id/15762. Broadsides are single sheets of paper, printed on one side, to be read unfolded. They carried public information such as proclamations as well as ballads and news of the day. Cheaply available, pedlars and chapmen sold them on the streets. They offer a valuable insight into many aspects of the society they were published in, and the National Library of Scotland holds over 250,000 of them.

Broggi, M.

2001 *Memòries d'un cirurgià*. Barcelona: Edicions 62.

2005 *Anys de plenitud. Memòries d'un cirugià*. Barcelona: Edicions 62.

Bueltzingsloewen, I. von

1997 *Machines à instruire, machines à guérir. Les hôpitaux universitaires et la medicalisation de la société allemande 1730-1850*. Lyon: Presses Universitaires de Lyon.

Campo, R.

1998 *The desire to heal*. New York: Norton.

Castel, R.

1976 *L'Ordre Psychiatrique. L'Age d'or de l'aliénisme*. París: Les Editions de Minuit.

Comelles, J. M.

1988 *La razón y la sinrazón. Asistencia psiquiátrica y desarrollo del Estado en la España Contemporánea*. Barcelona: PPU.

1991 Psychiatric care in relation to the development of the contemporary state: The case of Catalonia. *Culture, Medicine and Psychiatry* 15, 2: 193-217.

1996 Da superstizioni a medicina popolare: La transizione da un concetto religioso a un concetto médico. AM. *Rivista della Società Italiana di Antropologia Médica* 1-2: 57-89.

1998 Parole de médecin. Le récit sur la pratique dans la médecine contemporaine. In: F. Laplantine, J. Lévy, J.B. Martin, A. Nouss (eds.) *Récit et connaissance*. Lyon: Presses Universitaires de Lyon, pp. 299-316.

2000 The role of local knowledge in medical practice: A trans-historical perspective. *Culture, Medicine and Psychiatry* 24: 41-75.

2004 Fiebres, médicos y visitadores. Notas etnográficas sobre la práctica médica durnate el franquismo". In J. Martínez-Pérez, I. Porras Gallo, P. Samblás Tilve, M. del Cura González (eds.) *La medicina ante el nuevo*

*Milenio: una perspectiva histórica*. Albacete: Ediciones de la Universidad Castilla-La Mancha, pp. 989-1018.

Danés, M.

1978 *Cinquanta anys de medicina rural.* Sant Celoni. Ajuntament de Sant Celoni. Imprenta Bilbeny.

Diasio, N.

1999 *La science impure. Anthropologie et médecine en France, Grande-Bretagne, Italie, Pays-Bas*. Paris: Presses Universitaires de France.

Fabrega Jr., H.

1974 *Disease and Social Behavior*. Cambridge: M.I.T. Press.

Flores, G.

2002 Mad scientists, compassionate healers, and greedy egotists: the portrayal of physicians in the movies. *Journal of the National Medical Association* 94, 7: 635-58.

2004 Doctors in the movies. *Archives of Disease and Childhood* 89: 1084-1088.

Freidson, E.

1978 [1970] *La profesión médica*. Barcelona: Península.

Foucault, M.

1978 [1963] *Naissance de la clinique*. Paris: Presses Universitaires de France.

Galam, E. (ed.)

1996 *Infiniment médecins. Les généralistes entre la science et l'humain.* Paris: Autrement.

García Ballester, L.; McVaughn, M. R.; Rubio Vela, A.

1989 *Medical licensing and learning in fourteenth-century Valencia*. Philadelphia: American Philosophical Society.

Gawande, A.

2003 *Complicacions*. Barcelona: Empúries.

Gelfand, T.

1981 The decline of the ordinary practitioner and the rise of a modern medical profession. In: M.S. Staum, D.E. Larsen (eds.) *Doctors, patients, and society. Power and authority in medical care.* Calgary, Ma: Wilfrid Laurier University Press, pp. 105-132.

Goldstein, J.

1997 [1987] *Consoler et classifier. L'essor de la psychiatrie française*. Le Plessis- Robinson: Institut Synthélabo.

Groopman, J.

1997 *The measure of our days. A spiritual exploration of illness*. Penguin.

Gross, S.D.

1875 *The glory and the hardships of the medical life being the valedictory adress delivered at the Philadelphia Academic of Music. March 11 1875 before the trustees, faculty and students of the Jefferson Medical College at his forty-ninth annual commencement*. Philadelphia, P: Madeira Surgical Instrument Maker.

Helman, C. G.

1978 "Feed a cold, starve a fever". Folk models of infection in an English suburban community, and their relation to medical treatment. *Culture, Medicine and Psychiatry* 2, 2: 107-139.

2004 *Suburban shaman. A journey through medicine*. Cape Town: Double Storey.

Hilfiker, D.

1985 *Not all of us are saints. A doctor'sjourney with the poor.* New York: Hill and Wang.

2003 *Healing the wounds. A physician looks at his work.* Omaha: Creighton.

Hipócrates de Cos

1986 *Tratados Hipocráticos II. De los aires, las aguas y los lugares. Sobre los humores. Sobre los flatos. Predicciones I. Predicciones II. Premoniciones de Cos.* Madrid: Editorial Gredos.

Kee, H. C.

1992 *Medicina, Milagro y Magia en tiempos del Nuevo Testamento.* Cordoba: El Almendro.

Klass, P.

1987 *A not entirely benign procedure.* New York: Plume.

Konner, M.

1988 *Becoming a doctor: A journey of initiation in medical school.* Nueva York: Penguin Books.

Laín Entralgo, P.

1998 [1950] *La historia clínica. Historia y teoría del relato patográfico.* Madrid: Triacastela.

1964 *La relación médico-enfermo. Historia y Teoría.* Madrid: Revista de Occidente.

1976 *Descargo de Conciencia (1930-1960).* Barcelona: Barral Editores.

1984 Antropologia médica para clínicos. Barcelona: Salvat.

1987 *La curación por la palabra en la Antigüedad Clásica.* Barcelona: Anthropos

Lesage, A.-R.

1980 *Gil Blas de Santillana*. Barcelona: Círculo de Amigos del Libro.

Littré, E.

1875 *Médecine et médecins*. París: Librairie Académique Didier et Compagnie.

López Terrada, M. L.; Martínez Vidal, A. (eds.)

1996 Monográfico: El Tribunal del Real Protomedicato en la Monarquía Hispánica 1593-1808. *Dynamis* 16. (Granada, Universidad de Granada).

Menéndez, E. L.

1978 El modelo médico y la salud de los trabajadores. In: F. Basaglia et al., *La salud de los trabajadores*. México, DF: Nueva Imagen, pp. 11-53.

1990 *Antropología Médica. Orientaciones, desigualdades y transacciones*. México, DF: CIESAS.

Morán, G.

1998 *El Maestro en el erial. Ortega y Gasset y la cultura del Franquismo*. Barcelona: Tusquets.

Munaret, Le Docteur

1840 *Du Médecin des villes et du medecin de campagne. Moeurs et Science, par le Docteur....* Paris: Germer-Baillière, Libraire Editeur.

Parsons, T.

1984 *El sistema social*. Madrid: Alianza Editorial.

Perdiguero, E.

1997 Healing alternatives in Alicante, Spain, in the late nineteenth and twentieth centuries. In M. Gijswijt-Höfstrat, H. Marland & H. de Waardt (eds.) *Illness and healing alternatives in Western Europe*. London: Routledge, pp. 205-223.

2002 Con medios humanos y divinos: la lucha contra la enfermedad y la muerte en el Alicante del siglo XVIII. *Dynamis* 22: 121-150.

Pla, A.N.

2000 *Memóries d'un metge*. Andorra la Vella: Edicions DdA.

Porter, D. & Porter, R.

1989 *Patient's progress. Doctors and doctoring in eigteenth-century England.* Cambridge: Polity Press.

Risse, G. B.

1999 *Mending bodies, saving souls*. Oxford: Oxford University Press.

Rosenberg, Ch. E.

1986 *The care of strangers. The rise of America's hospital system*. New York: Basic Books.

1992 The therapeutic revolution: Medicine, meaning, and social change in nineteenth-century America. In: Ch. E. Rosenberg (ed.) *Explaining epidemics and other essays.* Cambridge: Cambridge University Press, pp. 9-31.

Turow, J.

1988 *Playing doctor. Television, storytelling and medical powe*r. New York: Oxford University Press.

Tuthill, F. M.D.

1855 *First years of practice. An adress to the graduating class of the New York Medical College*. New York: Edward P. Allen.

Velázquez, M. D.

1987 *Estudio de Comunidad Zinciro, Michoacan*. México, DF: IMSS-COPLAMAR.

Verghese, A.

1994 *My own country. A doctor'sstory*. New York: Vintage Books.

Vogel, M. J.

1980 *The invention of modern hospital. Boston 1870-1930*. Chicago: University of Chicago Press.

1989 Managing medicine: creating a profession of hospital administration in the United States 1895-1915". In: L. Granshaw & R. Porter (eds.) *The hospital in history*. London: Routledge, pp 243-260.

Ware, J.

1849 *Duties and qualifications of physicians. An introductory lecture*. London: John Henry Parker.

1851 *Success in the medical profession. An introductory lecture*. Boston: David Clapp, Printer.

Winckler, M.

2000 [1998] *La maladie de Sachs*. Paris: Editions J'ai lu.

Zarzoso, A.

2001 El pluralismo médico a través de la correspondencia privada en la Cataluña del siglo XVIII". *Dynamis* 21: 141-159.

## Contributors

**Sylvie Fainzang** is an anthropologist, senior researcher in the Inserm (Institut national de la santé et de la recherché médicale) and member of the Cermes (Centre de recherche médecine, sciences, santé et société). Her present research relates to information and lying in the doctor/patient relationship. She is the author of: *L'intérieur des choses. Maladie, divination et reproduction sociale chez les Bisa du Burkina* (L'Harmattan 1986), *Pour une anthropologie de la maladie en France. Un regard africaniste* (EHESS 1989), *La femme de mon mari. Etude ethnologique du mariage polygamique en Afrique et en France* (L'Harmattan, 1988), *Ethnologie des anciens alcooliques. La liberté ou la mort* (Presses Universitaires de France 1996), *Médicaments et société. Le patient, le médecin et l'ordonnance* (Presses Universitaires de France 2001), *Médecins, malades, information et mensonge* (Presses Universitaires de France 2006). Contact: sylvie.fainzang@wanadoo.fr

**Els van Dongen** is medical anthropologist and senior staff member of the Department of Anthropology & Sociology and the Amsterdam School for Social Science Research of the University of Amsterdam. She is chair of the Medical Anthropology at Home network in Europe. She is editor of the Dutch journal Medische Antropologie and member of the editorial board of Anthropology & Medicine and AM Revista della Societá Italiana di Antropologia Medica. She published on mental health issues, migrants and refugees, chronic illness, social memory, elderly, trauma and violence. She is the author of *Walking stories. An oddnography of mad people's work with culture* (Rosenberg 2002), *Worlds of psychotic people* (Routledge 2004), *Lying & illness. Power and performance* (Spinhuis 2005, together with S. Fainzang). Contact: elsvdongen@planet.nl

**Ruth Kutalek** is medical anthropologist and assistant professor at the Unit Ethnomedicine and International Health, Institute for the History of Medicine, Center for Public Health, Medical University of Vienna and lecturer at the Department of Social and Cultural Anthropology, University of Vienna. She has done fieldwork in Tanzania, Uganda, Ethiopia and Vienna; her main fields of interests are ethnomedicine and medical anthropology (indigenous therapies and aetiologies, lay aetiologies, medical pluralism, divination); ethnopharmacology and ethnobotany (esp. indigenous strategies of conserving biodiversity) and museum anthropology (paintings from Tanzania and

Congo). She is co-editor of the Viennese Ethnomedicine Newsletter and member of the editorial board of Curare. Contact: ruth.kutalek @meduniwien.ac.at

**Armin Prinz** is Professor at the Unit Ethnomedicine and International Health, Institute for the History of Medicine, Center for Public Health, Medical University of Vienna. He has done fieldwork in DR Congo, Senegal, Uganda and Ethiopia and has spent over four years among the Azande on the border DR Congo and Sudan. His main interests are ethnomedicine/medical anthropology (traditional medicine and health structures, traditional therapy among the Azande, local aetiologies, portraits of traditional healers) nutritional anthropology (health and demographic implications of diet change esp. cassava, food choices, obesity), ethnopharmacology (antimicrobial properties of local remedies, Cinchona, Rauwolfia, oracle poisons), history of medicine (van Swieten, Bremser, Piso); tropical medicine and travel medicine (Lyme disease, Diabetes mellitus, trypanosomiasis, HIV, thrombosis). Besides having published more than hundred articles and films in this field, he works as an emergency physician at the Vienna International Airport. Contact: armin.prinz@meduniwien.ac.at

**Hishamah Bel Khodja** has a M.Sc. in medical anthropology from the University of Amsterdam. She graduated with a thesis on refugee women: *"Give me your ears!" Seeking refuge from sexual violence: Further hearings in the Netherlands*. She also studied transpersonal psychology at the New Seed Sanctuary in Philadelphia. As an anthropologist she works with an "activist" and applied perspective and is currently involved in the organisation of the European Feminist Forum. Her special interests are women studies, sexual violence and human rights.

**Marianne Cense** is an expert in the field of domestic violence, sexual harassment and sexual abuse. She studied innovation & gender studies and has a European Master degree in interculturalisation of psychosocial healthcare. She works as a researcher, trainer and advisor on sexual and domestic violence since 1993 at TransAct, the Dutch national NGO on domestic and sexual violence and issues of gender and ethnicity. She is co-ordinator of projects concerning the improvement of prevention strategies and healthcare for victims of violence, with a special interest in clients from different ethnic backgrounds and refugees. Contact: m.cense@transact.nl

**Janus Oomen** is doctor in internal medicine with a Ph.D. on liver diseases. He worked as associate professor in disease nosology and computer assisted education, University of Amsterdam, internist consultant in psychiatry, and lecturer in psychiatric specialist training programs. Recently he received a Master degree in medical anthropology. From 2002 he is as postdoc affiliated to the International Amsterdam Masters Medical Anthropology (AMMA). Since 1995 he is active as volunteer for Amnesty International in the Medical Examination Group, as medical examiner and in the coordinating body. Contact: oomen@xs4-all.nl

**Annemiek Richters** is professor of culture, health and illness, Department Public Health and Primary Care, Leiden University Medical Center. Her background is medicine, anthropology, sociology and philosophy. Her research has focused on topics such as: gender violence, trauma, and healing; western medicine and women's body politics in the context of globalization; multicultural medicine; reproductive health of migrant women in the Netherlands; socio-cultural aspects of HIV/AIDS. She is particularly interested in issues in the field of gender, health and human rights in the context of (post-) conflict societies. Contact: j.m.richters@lumc.nl

**Marian Tankink** is a community psychiatric nurse and medical anthropologist. She works on her PhD at the Department of Public Health and Primary Care, Leiden University Medical Center. Her thesis will focus on the results of her research among refugee women in the Netherlands, who experienced sexual violence as part of the conflict in their countries of origin (Afghanistan, Bosnia or South-Sudan) or during their flight. In this research she is primarily interested in the differences and similarities in meaning production and health-seeking strategies among women who fled from Afghanistan, Bosnia or South-Sudan. Contact: m.t.a.tankink@lumc.nl

**Charlotte Bredahl Jacobsen** holds a PhD degree from the Department of Anthropology, University of Copenhagen, Denmark. Since 2001 she has been working with (trans)cultural psychiatry in Denmark. Currently she holds a position as project manager at DSI Danish Institute for Health Services Research. Contact: cbj@dsi.dk

**Jónina Einarsdóttir** is associate professor in anthropology at the University of Iceland. She completed her PhD in social anthropology from Stockholm University 2000. Her main fields of research are anthropology of children, medical anthropology and development studies. She has fieldwork experience from Guinea-Bissau (1993-98) on which she bases her book *Tired of weeping. Mother love, child death and poverty*. Since 2001 Einarsdóttir has conducted research on ethical questions related to treatment of infants born with birth weight 1000 g or less and the implications of their birth on daily life of their families in Iceland. Contact: je@hi.is

**Josep M. Comelles** (Barcelona 1949), M.Sc. Ph.D Medicine (UB), Ph.D. Anthropology (EHESS; Paris), M.A. Psychology (Psicologia, UB), Psychiatrist. Fields of Research: medical anthropology, history of science, science studies. Areas: Europe. Main interests: migration and health, cultural psychiatry, public policies. Post. Full Professor (Universitat Rovira i Virgili, Tarragona, Spain). Visiting Professor: CIESAS, Mexico; Université Paris X, Nanterre; Université Lumière-Lyon. Author of several books like *La razón y la sinrazón. Asistencia psiquiátrica y desarrollo del Estado en la España Contemporánea.* (PPU 1988), and *Stultifera Navis. La Locura, el poder y la ciudad.* (Milenio 2006), and of articles, "Psychiatric care in relation to the development of the contemporary state: The case of Catalonia", *Culture, Medicine and Psychiatry* 15, 2: 193-217, 1991, "The role of local knowledge in medical practice: A trans-historical perspective" *Culture, Medicine and Psychiatry* 24: 41-75, 2000. "Writing at the margin of the margin: medical anthropology in Southern Europe", *Anthropology & Medicine* 9, 1: 7-23, 2002, and "Medicine, magic and religion in a hospital ward. An anthropologist as patient", In: J. M. Comelles & E. van Dongen (eds.) *Themes in Medical Anthropology.* (Fondazione Angelo Celli Argo 2002). Contact: josep-comelles@gmail.com

## R



## S



## T



## U



## V



## W

## Medizinkulturen im Vergleich

hrsg. von Rolf Wirsing und Beatrix Pfleiderer

Gitta Bach
**Zwischen Staatsideologie und Islam: Malaiische Medizin in Singapore**
Bd. 1, 1992, 248 S., 17,90 €, br., ISBN 3-89473-236-9

Christine Tuschinsky
**Produktion, Handel und Konsumtion nicht-westlicher Medikamente in Südost-Asien: Malaiische *jamu* in Singapore**
Bd. 2, 1992, 224 S., 17,90 €, br., ISBN 3-89473-237-7

Sibylle Hielscher
**Heiler in Mali**
Ein Beitrag zur postkolonialen Afrikanischen Medizin
Bd. 4, 1992, 250 S., 17,90 €, br., ISBN 3-89473-196-6

Johannes Sommerfeld
**Körper, Krise und Vodou**
Eine Studie zur Kreolmedizin und Gesundheitsversorgung in Haiti
Bd. 5, 1994, 203 S., 17,90 €, br., ISBN 3-89473-198-2

Dunja Moeller
**Sanfte Medizin**
Eine medizinanthropologische Untersuchung zur Umsetzung der anthroposophischen Medizin in den klinischen Alltag
Bd. 6, 1993, 288 S., 17,90 €, br., ISBN 3-89473-249-0

Ute Schumann
**Homöopathie in der modernen indischen Gesundheitsversorgung: Ein Medium kultureller Kontinuität**
Bd. 7, 1992, 250 S., 24,90 €, br., ISBN 3-89473-536-8

Flavien Tiokou Ndonko
**Représentations culturelles des Excréments**
Étude comparative des déchets du corps chez les populations de la savane et de la côte du Cameroun
Bd. 8, 1993, 352 S., 35,90 €, br., ISBN 3-89473-578-3

Gabriele Förster
**Homöopathie und Krankheitserleben: Die Suche nach dem Sinn**
Bd. 9, 1993, 288 S., 19,90 €, br., ISBN 3-89473-580-5

Renate Schukies
**Red Hat**
Cheyenne Blue Sky Maker and Keeper of the Sacred Arrows
Bd. 10, 1993, 452 S., 22,90 €, br., ISBN 3-89473-585-6

Petra Wehmeyer
**Das ayurvedische Heilmittel Liv. 52**
Eine Untersuchung seiner Bestandteile und Wirkmechanismen aus systemimmanenter Perspektive auf der Grundlage der "brhattrayi"
Bd. 11, 1993, 152 S., 17,90 €, br., ISBN 3-89473-523-6

Elisabeth Grüner
**Die Pflanze als Phytotherapeutikum**
Anspruch und Wirklichkeit innerhalb des WHO-Programms "Gesundheit für alle bis zum Jahr 2000" und ihre Bedeutung in der modernen und traditionalen Medizin Deutschlands
Bd. 12, 1993, 128 S., 15,90 €, br., ISBN 3-89473-760-3

Annette Leibing
**Blick auf eine verrückte Welt**
Kultur und Psychiatrie in Brasilien
Bd. 13, 1995, 150 S., 15,90 €, br., ISBN 3-8258-2298-2

Joyce Dreezens-Fuhrke
**Behinderung als Zeichen**
Soziokultureller Umgang mit Behinderung in einer javanischen Gesellschaft zwischen Tradition und Gegenwart
Bd. 15, 1996, 304 S., 24,90 €, br., ISBN 3-8258-2463-2

Lilo Roost Vischer
**Alltägliche Tote**
Ethnologische Untersuchungen in einem Bestattungsinstitut und einem Krematorium in der Schweiz
Bd. 16, 1999, 112 S., 15,90 €, br., ISBN 3-8258-3500-6

Elsbeth Kneuper
**Tod, Weiblichkeit, Repräsentation**
Forschen in einem deutschen Bestattungsinstitut
Bd. 17, 1999, 88 S., 15,90 €, br., ISBN 3-8258-4264-9

LIT Verlag GmbH & Co. KG Wien

Auslieferung Österreich: Medienlogistik Pichler-ÖBZ GmbH & Co KG
IZ-NÖ Süd, Straße 1, Objekt 34, A-2355 Wiener Neudorf, Postfach 133
Tel. +43 (0) 2236/63 535 - 290, Fax +43 (0) 2236/63 535 - 243, e-Mail: bestellen@medien-logistik.at

Auslieferung Deutschland: Fresnostr. 2 48159 Münster
Tel.: 0251 – 62 03 222 – Fax 0251 – 23 19 72
e-Mail: vertrieb@lit-verlag.de – http://www.lit-verlag.de

## Medizinkulturen im Vergleich

hrsg. von Rolf Wirsing und Beatrix Pfleiderer

Sabine Heß

**Nahrungsmeidung und Vegetarismus**

Konzepte und Kontexte von Nahrungsauswahl am Beispiel von Vegetariern in Süddeutschland

Mediziner und Ernährungswissenschaftler beschreiben bei Studien mit Vegetariern immer wieder deren Ausnahmen – wie z. B. Fisch – als problematisch. Diese Personen definierten sich als Vegetarier, seien aber gar keine "richtigen". Mit Hilfe eines sozialwissenschaftlichen Ansatzes zeigt dieses Buch auf, welche Konzepte und Kontexte der heutigen Eßkultur in Deutschland zugrunde liegen. Der freiwillige Vegetarismus ist hierbei nur eine von vielen Ernährungsweisen, welche in dem größeren Zusammenhang der Lebensstile gesehen werden muß. Die auf qualitativen Interviews beruhende Selbstdarstellung von Vegetariern und deren Integration von Fisch- und Fleischausnahmen, die ihrer Identität als "richtige Vegetarier" keinen Abbruch tut, führt die Komplexität der Identitätsfrage und des menschlichen Handelns vor Augen.

Bd. 18, 2000, 96 S., 10,90 €, br., ISBN 3-8258-4458-7

Angelika Wolf; Viola Hörbst (Hg.)

**Medizin und Globalisierung**

Universelle Ansprüche – lokale Antworten

Die Biomedizin erhebt den Anspruch globaler Gültigkeit. Die unter dem Begriff der Globalisierung und Globalität diskutierten weltumspannenden Ströme von Ideen, Technologien, Praktiken und Menschen sind im letzten Jahrzehnt vorrangig hinsichtlich der Bereiche von Ökonomie, neuen Medien und Migration untersucht worden. Die Bedeutung von Globalisierungsprozessen in Bereichen der Medizin und Gesundheit wurden hingegen bislang wenig bearbeitet. Dieser Band versammelt Beiträge, die anhand von ethnologischen Feldstudien und theoretischen Auseinandersetzungen aufzeigen, dass die Biomedizin mit ihrem globalen Anspruch einer Wandlung im kulturellen Kontext unterzogen wird. Dabei modifizieren lokale Akteure biomedizische Konzepte und passen sie den örtlichen Gegebenheiten an. Im Spannungsfeld zwischen globalen Ansprüchen und lokalem Handeln werden Modelle verändert und indigenisiert. Dadurch gewinnt auch im medizinischen Bereich das Lokale an Bestand und widersetzt sich einer Homogenisierung. Der Band leistet einen Beitrag zum Diskurs um Globalisierung in der Medical Anthropology.

Bd. 19, 2003, 240 S., 15,90 €, br., ISBN 3-8258-5655-0

Jutta Gruber

**Der Animalische Magnetismus – zwischen Abwehr und Begeisterung**

Eine ideengeschichtliche Untersuchung

Der Aspektreichtum des Animalischen Magnetismus Franz Anton Mesmers wird auf dem Hintergrund dieser ideengeschichtlichen Untersuchung in faszinierender Weise sichtbar. Der wissenschaftstheoretische Rahmen im Sinne Thomas S. Kuhns hilft zu verstehen, warum das Phänomen "Mesmerismus" soviele Menschen begeisterte und und überzeugte und gleichzeitig soviele Angst und Ablehnung auslöste. Diese multidisziplinäre Arbeit zeigt in spannender Weise die kontextuellen Ursachen für den enormen Erfolg dieses Heilverfahrens in seiner Zeit. Darüber hinaus gibt sie Hinweise auf die strukturellen Schwierigkeiten, denen sich "Außenseitermethoden" stellen müssen.

Bd. 20, Frühjahr 2007, ca. 88 S., ca. 10,90 €, br., ISBN 3-8258-5669-0

Christoph Imhof

**Von Alkaloid zu Osaín**

Die *Medicina verde* in Kuba im Kontext von Staat und Gesellschaft. Eine Spurensuche in Havanna

Die Nutzung der Heilpflanzen hat in den letzten Jahren im kubanischen Gesundheitswesen an Bedeutung gewonnen. Auch von Seiten der Anhänger afrokubanischer Religionen ist eine grosse Nachfrage nach Heilpflanzen feststellbar. Eingebettet in einen historischen und wirtschaftspolitischen Kontext wird im Buch anhand von Gesprächen mit Funktionären des Gesundheitsministeriums, mit Gärtnern, Heilpflanzenverkäufern und Eingeweihten afrokubanischer Religionen, ein Bogen von einer schulmedizinisch motivierten Verwendung der Pflanzen bis hin zur religiös motivierten Verwendung gespannt.

Bd. 21, 2002, 208 S., 17,90 €, br., ISBN 3-8258-5871-5

LIT Verlag GmbH & Co. KG Wien

Auslieferung Österreich: Medienlogistik Pichler-ÖBZ GmbH & Co KG
IZ-NÖ Süd, Straße 1, Objekt 34, A-2355 Wiener Neudorf, Postfach 133
Tel. +43 (0) 2236/63 535 - 290, Fax +43 (0) 2236/63 535 - 243, e-Mail: bestellen@medien-logistik.at

Auslieferung Deutschland: Fresnostr. 2 48159 Münster
Tel.: 0251 – 62 03 222 – Fax 0251 – 23 19 72
e-Mail: vertrieb@lit-verlag.de – http://www.lit-verlag.de

**Indus**

Ethnologische Südasien-Studien

hrsg. von Prof. Dr. Frank Heidemann (München), Prof. Dr. Georg Pfeffer (Berlin) und Prof. Dr. William Sax (Heidelberg)

Tina Otten

**HEILUNG DURCH RITUALE**

Vom Umgang mit Krankheit bei den Ronā im Hochland Orissas

Indus

LIT

Tina Otten

**Heilung durch Rituale**

Vom Umgang mit Krankheit bei den Rona im Hochland Orissas

Der Umgang mit Gesundheit und Krankheit bei den Rona unterscheidet sich von anderen bekannten Medizinen Indiens wie Ayurveda, Unani oder Siddha. Die meisten Krankheiten, die die Rona kennen, können nur durch Rituale geheilt werden. Die soziale Relevanz einer Krankheit und die Art der Verwandschaft bestimmen, welcher Heiler oder Heilerin behandeln darf. Mit dieser Monographie wird eine differenzierte Analyse einer mittelindischen Gemeinschaft vorgelegt, die sich von Hindu-Gesellschaften deutlich unterscheidet.

Bd. 9, 2006, 440 S., 34,90 €, br., ISBN 3-8258-9395-2

LIT Verlag GmbH & Co. KG Wien

Auslieferung Österreich: Medienlogistik Pichler-ÖBZ GmbH & Co KG
IZ-NÖ Süd, Straße 1, Objekt 34, A-2355 Wiener Neudorf, Postfach 133
Tel. +43 (0) 2236/63 535 - 290, Fax +43 (0) 2236/63 535 - 243, e-Mail: bestellen@medien-logistik.at

Auslieferung Deutschland: Fresnostr. 2 48159 Münster
Tel.: 0251 – 62 03 222 – Fax 0251 – 23 19 72
e-Mail: vertrieb@lit-verlag.de – http://www.lit-verlag.de

## Worte – Werke – Utopien

Thesen und Texte Münsterscher Gelehrter

A. Fiedermutz-Laun; F. Pera; E. T. Peuker; F. Diederich (Hg.)

**Zur Akzeptanz von Magie, Religion und Wissenschaft**

Ein medizinethnologisches Symposium der Institute für Ethnologie und Anatomie, Westfälische Wilhelms-Universität Münster 1999

"Zur Akzeptanz von Magie, Religion und Wissenschaft -- ein medizinethnologisches Symposium´´ ist das Thema einer interdisziplinären Tagung von Ethnologie und Anatomie, die Vertreter aus elf Instituten der Westfälischen Wilhelms-Universität Münster und Gastvortragende aus anderen Universitäten zusammenführt. In diesem Brückenschlag zwischen Natur- und Geisteswissenschaft diskutieren Gelehrte aus der Sicht ihrer jeweiligen Disziplin historische, theologische, psychologische, religionswissenschaftliche, medizinische und ethnologische Ansätze und beziehen auch die alltägliche Praxis ein. Dass die Trennung von Magie, Religion und Wissenschaft nicht mehr uneingeschränkt zu rechtfertigen ist, da diese Bereiche im Leben des Einzelnen wie in allen Kulturen zusammenwirken, dass sie jedoch im Verlauf historischer Prozesse unterschiedlich „virulent" in Erscheinung treten – diese und weitere Ergebnisse werden in der lebhaften Schlussdiskussion deutlich. Die Vorträge sind in diesem Tagungsband zusammengefasst. Auf dem Umschlag charakterisiert "Der Sündenfall´´ aus der Schedelschen Weltchronik (1493, Ausschnitt) das Neben- und Miteinander von "Magie, Religion und Wissenschaft´´: die magische Vorstellung von der heilkräftigen Wirkung des Drachenbaumes, das religiöse Thema von der Vertreibung des Menschen aus dem Paradies und -- der "Apfel der Erkenntnis´´.

Bd. 17, 2002, 392 S., 35,90 €, gb., ISBN 3-8258-5211-3

## Interethnische Beziehungen und Kulturwandel

Ethnologische Beiträge zu soziokultureller Dynamik

hrsg. von Prof. Dr. Jürgen Jensen (Universität Hamburg)

Ulrich Schulz-Burgdorf

**Aspekte der Swahili Volksmedizin im Lamu-Archipel Kenyas**

Ein historischer Abriß führt in Wandlungsprozesse in Swahili-Stadtgesellschaften der ostafrikanischen Küste ein und zu den gegenwärtigen Verhältnissen in der Kleinregion hin. Der systematische Teil geht auf magisch-rituelle und somatisch-kurative Praktiken ein. Dieser letztgenannte Heilkundetyp mit seinen naturalistischen Ätiologien und Bezügen zur graeco-arabischen *Tibb*- Medizin ist (wie nicht-rituelle Therapien generell) lange von der Küstenforschung vernachlässigt worden. Dieser Komplex wird anhand von Feldmaterial dargestellt, wobei die Monetarisierung therapeutischer Dienstleistungen im urbanen Milieu aufgezeigt wird – ein Vorgang, bei dem neuartige literale Wissensressourcen und kaufmännisch-kalkulatorische Strategien ins Spiel kommen und Elemente verschiedener Medizinsysteme verarbeitet werden. Die Arbeit bildet den ersten Teil einer Feldstudie, die den Gegenstand *Utabibu*-Heilkunde unter den ethnopharmakologischen und wirtschaftsethnologischen Gesichtspunkten "Indigenisierung" bzw. "Professionalisierung/Kommerzialisierung" behandelt.
Past and present processes of social change shaping Swahili urban societies of the East African coast and especially the area of study are outlined. Ritual manipulation and somatically-related curing procedures form the central theme of the thesis. The last-mentioned type of curing based on naturalistic etiology and elements of the graeco-bactric *tibb*-system of medicine has long been neglected in coastal research. In the use of field data the monetarization of therapeutic services in the urban sector is emphasized: a process amalgamating literal knowledge resources, elements of different medical systems and special economic strategies. The thesis is the first part of a continued field study dedicated to *utabibu*-medicine in which combined approaches of ethnopharmacology and economic anthropology center around indigenization and professionalization/commercialization.

Bd. 7, 1994, 128 S., 17,90 €, br., ISBN 3-89473-649-6

LIT Verlag GmbH & Co. KG Wien

Auslieferung Österreich: Medienlogistik Pichler-ÖBZ GmbH & Co KG
IZ-NÖ Süd, Straße 1, Objekt 34, A-2355 Wiener Neudorf, Postfach 133
Tel. +43 (0) 2236/63 535 - 290, Fax +43 (0) 2236/63 535 - 243, e-Mail: bestellen@medien-logistik.at

Auslieferung Deutschland: Fresnostr. 2 48159 Münster
Tel.: 0251 – 62 03 222 – Fax 0251 – 23 19 72
e-Mail: vertrieb@lit-verlag.de – http://www.lit-verlag.de

# Medizingeschichte

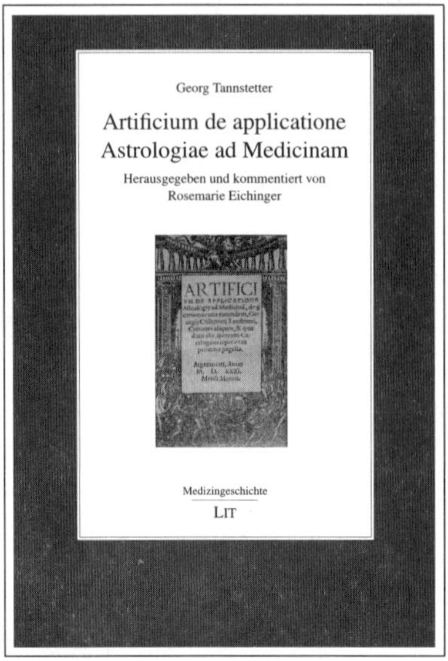

Georg Tannstetter
**Artificium de applicatione Astrologiae ad Medicinam**
Herausgegeben und kommentiert von Rosemarie Eichinger

In dieser Arbeit wird eine außergewöhnliche Quelle vorgestellt, die ein Schlaglicht auf die Bedeutung der Astrologie in den Lehrplänen der Universitäten wirft. Im Jahre 1526 hielt der humanistische Naturwissenschafter, Lehrer und Arzt Georg Tannstetter die iatromathematische Vorlesung mit dem Titel „Artificium de applicatione Astrologiae ad Medicinam" an der Medizinischen Fakultät der Universität Wien. Diese gedruckte Vorlesungsmitschrift wird nun im Rahmen eimer kritischen Edition nebst Übersetzung und Kommentar erstmals im vollständigen Wortlaut vorgelegt.

Bd. 1, 2006, 288 S., 24,90 €, br., ISBN 3-8258-9540-8

Jörg Vögele; Heiner Fangerau; Thorsten Noack (Hg..)
**Geschichte der Medizin – Geschichte in der Medizin**
Forschungsthemen und Perspektiven

Die Medizin des 19., 20. und frühen 21. Jahrhunderts folgt mit ihrem Anspruch des Heilens, des Forschens und der Ausbildung von Ärztinnen und Ärzten einem gesellschaftlichen und historischen Wandel. Dieser hat Auswirkungen auf die Medizin als Wissenschaft, ihre Ethik und ihre Theorie. In diesem Sinn bedeutet „Medizin" immer auch ein Nach- und Nebeneinander unterschiedlicher Konzepte, Handlungsfelder und Verhaltensweisen. Der vorliegende Band stellt aktuelle Forschungen zur Geschichte, Theorie und Ethik der Medizin mit ihren Perspektiven für die Medizin des 21. Jahrhunderts exemplarisch dar.

Bd. 2, 2006, 240 S., 24,90 €, gb., ISBN 3-8258-9562-9

LIT Verlag GmbH & Co. KG Wien

Auslieferung Österreich: Medienlogistik Pichler-ÖBZ GmbH & Co KG
IZ-NÖ Süd, Straße 1, Objekt 34, A-2355 Wiener Neudorf, Postfach 133
Tel. +43 (0) 2236/63 535 - 290, Fax +43 (0) 2236/63 535 - 243, e-Mail: bestellen@medien-logistik.at

Auslieferung Deutschland: Fresnostr. 2 48159 Münster
Tel.: 0251 – 62 03 222 – Fax 0251 – 23 19 72
e-Mail: vertrieb@lit-verlag.de – http://www.lit-verlag.de